THE
CURRENCY
OF
LEADERSHIP

Bruce —
Thanks for making
work fun and not
drinking the Kool Aid!
Bill
1.15.2016

WILLIAM H. BISHOP

THE CURRENCY OF LEADERSHIP

TATE PUBLISHING
AND ENTERPRISES, LLC

The Currency of Leadership
Copyright © 2016 by William H. Bishop. All rights reserved.

No part of this publication may be reproduced, stored in a retrieval system or transmitted in any way by any means, electronic, mechanical, photocopy, recording or otherwise without the prior permission of the author except as provided by USA copyright law.

Scriptures taken from the Holy Bible, *New International Version*®, NIV®. Copyright © 1973, 1978, 1984 by Biblica, Inc.™ Used by permission of Zondervan. All rights reserved worldwide. www.zondervan.com

This book is designed to provide accurate and authoritative information with regard to the subject matter covered. This information is given with the understanding that neither the author nor Tate Publishing, LLC is engaged in rendering legal, professional advice. Since the details of your situation are fact dependent, you should additionally seek the services of a competent professional.

The opinions expressed by the author are not necessarily those of Tate Publishing, LLC.

Published by Tate Publishing & Enterprises, LLC
127 E. Trade Center Terrace | Mustang, Oklahoma 73064 USA
1.888.361.9473 | www.tatepublishing.com

Tate Publishing is committed to excellence in the publishing industry. The company reflects the philosophy established by the founders, based on Psalm 68:11,
"The Lord gave the word and great was the company of those who published it."

Book design copyright © 2016 by Tate Publishing, LLC. All rights reserved.
Cover design by Bill Francis Peralta
Interior design by Jomar Ouano

Published in the United States of America

ISBN: 978-1-68207-917-1
Education / Leadership
15.12.15

Other works by William H. Bishop

Going Home: A Networking Survival Guide

ACKNOWLEDGMENTS

I want to thank the people who have shared this journey with me over the past four years. Without them, I wouldn't have made it to the end. No one completes a doctorate on his own.

First and foremost, I want to thank God, the Alpha and Omega, King of kings and Lord of lords, and His son, Jesus Christ, my Lord and Savior, for leading me to Regent University back in 2008.

After completing my MBA and taking a year off, I started the Doctor of Philosophy in Organizational Leadership program. During the week of the first residency, I realized I was in the wrong program. On the last day of residency, I spoke with then Dean Winston about switching to the Doctor of Strategic Leadership program. Later that day, I made the switch and never looked back.

My journey to Regent and the pursuit of a doctorate began when I was in seventh grade. My parents and I had just started attending Tenth Presbyterian Church in Philadelphia, Pennsylvania, at the time. Dr. James M. Boice was the senior pastor, and he quickly became my unofficial mentor. I admired his academic achievements and prolific writing career. During the past year, I was listening to one of Dr. Boice's sermons in which he spoke about the doctrine of election. In the sermon, he mentioned that if God did not seek us first, we would never seek Him. He referenced a line in a hymn that stated, "I sought God seeking me." It was then I realized the seed for my doctoral journey had been planted all those years ago when I was at church. My doctoral journey had not occurred out of happenstance, nor was it due to my decision based on circumstances and opportunity. It was part of God's plan for my life. The curves and detours I took along the way were presumably necessary for the successful completion of the journey.

To my incredibly supportive wife, Barbara, and my twin daughters, Brooke and Megan, I extend my deepest thanks for their unwavering support, patience, and understanding. My wife is my greatest supporter and the biggest fan of my life. Thank you for walking beside me and taking this journey with me. I love you very, very, very much and look forward to the next leg of the journey.

Although they are not here to celebrate this achievement with me, I want to thank my parents for the sacrifices they made so I could have a quality education, which began at Grace Christian Academy and continued at Phil-Mont Christian Academy. My mother wanted nothing but the best for me and pushed me to excel academically. She instilled in me the belief that I could be anything I wanted and reach any goal. I miss you, Mom. I know you'd be proud. I am grateful to the Lord for allowing my father to live long enough to watch me cross the stage in 2010, when I graduated with my master's degree. Dad, even though you weren't formally educated, you were the smartest man I ever knew. Through your example, you taught me how to be a loving husband, a caring father, and a Christian. Thank you for being such a wonderful father, role model, and mentor.

My teacher at Grace Christian Academy, Donna Rineer, changed my life. She left a lasting impact on me. My days at Grace were the formidable days of my childhood. They laid the foundation of the person I am today. In large part, Donna was instrumental in the person I've become. She ingrained in me a love of learning and reading. Donna made learning fun and exciting, and she convinced me there was nothing I couldn't learn or do. When I left Grace to attend Phil-Mont Christian Academy, I had been setup for success by Donna. She instilled in me the motivation, drive, and ambition that allowed me to complete this incredible journey. Thank you, Donna, for your enthusiasm, encouragement, and believing in me when I didn't believe in myself. You were a special person and the true definition of what it means to be a teacher. I will never forget you and the influence you had on my life. One person *can* make a difference, and you made a difference in my life.

Dr. Gary Oster, thank you for the many conversations over coffee in which you guided me, supported me, encouraged me, and most of all, listened to me ramble. You were always willing to discuss ideas and provide feedback. During my time at Regent, you've been a mentor, professor, brother in Christ, and friend. Thank you for always being there and willing to lend an ear.

Thank you, Dr. Bramwell Osula, for the many discussions and e-mails over the past four years. Not only did you inspire me, you challenged me to set the bar higher and think beyond established boundaries. Your suggestions and seemingly simple words of advice were the fodder for critical thinking and in-depth analysis of complex ideas. I consider you a mentor and a friend.

And to my project chair, Dr. Kathleen Patterson, fittingly, you are indeed a servant of God. You were my first grading professor in the DSL program, during which, you complimented my writing, supported my ideas, and encouraged me to submit my articles for publication. From my first day in the program until the completion of my doctoral project, you provided enthusiastic support and sustained encouragement with an infectious positivity. It is appropriate that you are the chair for my final project. Thank you for chairing my project and walking the last few yards to the finish line with me.

To my fellow 2015 cohort members, Dr. Karen Bosler, Dr. Michael "Yama" Hoyes, and Dr. Mike Gorton, I couldn't have made it without you! We laughed together, endured together, critiqued each other, and prayed for one another. Your encouragement, support, motivation, and friendship made this journey fun, rewarding, and worthwhile. I thank each of you for carrying me when I was too weak to walk, pushing me when I needed a shove, and helping me up when I fell. I love all of you and thank God for bringing you into my life. I am a better person for knowing each of you. Carry on, doctors!

Thank you, David Boisselle, for taking the time to painstakingly edit this manuscript and make it better. Over the years, you've become my friend and a true brother in Christ. I deeply value your friendship, counsel, and advice. You are God's servant and never fail to put others first. In this world, Dave, you are a rare breed. I wouldn't have made it to the end of the journey without you. I am extremely grateful for your presence in my life.

Dr. Philip Foster, you were my guide on this journey. A year ahead in the program, you demonstrated the importance of reaching back to those in the first and second years. As I stated above, no one completes a doctorate on his own because it's a journey that must be undertaken with guidance from those who know the way. You knew the way and showed it to me, as well as others. I sincerely appreciate the words of advice, project reviews and suggestions, and encouragement to press on when the path didn't seem clear. Thank you for your friendship and for leading the way.

Master Chief Timothy Clemmons, my sea daddy, a master chief's master chief created in the master chief Billy Sunday mold. You led by example and walked your talk. Integrity was your mantra. You inspired others to be better than they ever thought possible, you opened locked doors, and you challenged me to not only meet the standard, but to set a new one. Your presence in my life has been one of mentorship, support, and friendship. Tim, you were an integral part of my life and leadership journey. I am a better leader due to your mentorship and example, and I am honored to have you as a friend and to be your fellow chief. "Once a Chief, always a Chief!"

The esteemed Dr. Corne Bekker, a remarkable scholar whose simple questions uncover amazingly complex truths and bits of wisdom. Thank you for your spiritual example and support. You are a brilliant man doing God's work. Your dedication to God is surpassed only by your service to His kingdom.

Lindsay Kennedy, thank you for reading this and injecting a woman's perspective. I sincerely appreciate your encouragement and enthusiasm throughout the completion of this manuscript. You'll make a great chief of staff someday!

And last but not least, to the 2015 PhD cohort members I began this journey with four years ago; Dr. Leana Polston-Murdoch, Dr. Joshua Henson, Dr. Timothy Brubaker, and Dr. Dave West, thank you for your continued friendship and support despite my change of direction. I am grateful I got to know each of you, and I value your friendship and presence in my life. God speed to all of you!

CONTENTS

Preface 17
Introduction 21
Day 1: Defining Values 33
    Agenda 33
    Values 37
    In the Beginning 49
    A Matter of Culture 59
    If the Situation Fits 69
    The Human Conscience 76
    Leadership Application 84
Day 2: Ethical Boundaries 87
    Defining Ethics and Their Purpose 87
    Litany of Failures 96
    Teaching Ethics 106
    Dilemmas 114
    A Greater Good 122
    Leadership Application 130

Day 3: Moral Standards 135
    Defining Morals 135
    Character 146
    Moral Behavior and the Law 152
    Natural Law, Moral Authority, and Responsibility ... 161
    The New Morality 169
    Leadership Application 175

Day 4: The Real Thing 179
    What is Authentic Leadership 179
    Integrity 190
    The Genuine Article 195
    Narcissism 206
    Groupthink 217
    Leadership Application 227

Day 5: The Power of Leadership 231
    Defining Leadership 231
    Power and Authority 241
    Leadership Styles 249
    Men versus Women 259
    Leadership Application 267
    Group Presentations 268
    Leadership Application 269

Epilogue 271
Afterword 283
Notes 285
About the Author 315

PREFACE

Organizations in the twenty-first century have been plagued by ethical failures. The egregious lapses in moral judgment and unethical behavior have dominated social media, the Internet, and twenty-four-hour-streaming news outlets. Corporations and organizations that were once bastions of core values have fallen prey to the wiles of misconduct and dishonesty. Once an ethical powerhouse whose values statement in their Code of Ethics boasted "commitments to communication, respect, integrity, and excellence,"[1] Enron's fall from grace was a wakeup call to the American people. The Enron debacle stands out as one of the most significant breaches of ethical conduct by an organization in the first decade of the twenty-first century. Its rapid ethical decline and fraudulent practices led to the implementation of new federal regulations. "In July of 2002, President Bush signed into law the Sarbanes-Oxley Act, intended to enhance corporate responsibility, enhance financial disclosures, and combat corporate and accounting fraud."[2]

In 2007, the subprime housing market crashed and nearly sent the nation's economy into a tailspin. In their exposé about the housing market collapse, *All the Devils Are Here* authors Bethany McLean and Joe Nocera noted, "Fraud was an everyday occurrence"[3] by many loan officers. Due to unethical practices in the housing financial industry, the government intervened in 2008 and provided a $700-billion bailout.

A Greycourt white paper noted: "In our view, poor risk controls, massive leverage, and the blind eye were really symptoms of a much worse disease: the root cause of the crisis was the gradual but ultimately complete collapse of *ethical behavior* (emphasis mine) across the financial industry. Once the financial industry came unmoored from its ethical base, financial firms were free to behave in ways that were in their—and especially their top executives'—short-term interest without any concern about the longer term impact on the industry's customers, on the broader American economy, or even on the firms' own employees. By a collapse of ethical behavior, we mean exactly what we say; that the actions of many—if not most—of the large American financial firms (and of the many foreign firms that succumbed to the American disease) would strike an ordinary person as unethical, repulsive, and scurrilous. But we also mean something more specific to the long-term viability of the financial industry, namely the disappearance of any sense of fiduciary responsibility to the ultimate client.

Integrity (emphasis mine) and a sense of responsibility to the industry's customers are at the core of what a financial industry must be all about; otherwise, it's just a big Ponzi scheme."[4]

The United States Armed Forces have also experienced a litany of ethical and leadership failures that has resulted in the firing of senior leaders, both officer and enlisted. Ethical shortcomings and misplaced values seemingly know no bounds.

The narrative that follows is the presentation of applied academic theory that addresses the issues of values alignment, ethical behavior, and moral boundaries in terms of leadership within the confines of an organization. While the story is fictitious, the academic content is not. The author's intention is to present a realistic scenario and address it through applied leadership theories and techniques in order to educate the reader and demonstrate a creative and innovative approach to learning and organizational improvement.

With the exception of the references to Master Chief Timothy Clemmons, USN (ret.) and Bill George, all characters appearing in this work are fictitious. Any resemblance to real persons, living or dead, is purely coincidental.

INTRODUCTION

As I prepared my introductory remarks for the company training that was now referred to as *The Leadership Academy,* I thought back over the events of the past ten months that had led to this moment. They were anything but glamorous. I'm Cheryl Stevens, CEO of the Company. I'm the first female CEO in the company's nearly one-hundred-year history. And I was nearly its last. Shortly after I had been installed as the CEO, the Company had experienced a litany of cascading leadership failures that shook it to its very core. Over the course of my tenure with the Company, I had risen from a junior vice president to the chief executive officer. Somewhere along the way, the Company had lost its moral compass.

When I was still a somewhat junior vice president, the chairwoman of the board approached me. Believing I was being asked to provide input for the next CEO to replace the retiring incumbent, I was very candid when asked what I would change about the Company. In fact, as I recall, I was quite brazen. My perception, particularly as a female, was that the Company had an infrastructure akin to a Good Old Boys Club that was built on a network dominated by vested senior managers. I was quite taken aback when I was informed I was to be the next chief executive officer. There were several vice presidents whose experience dwarfed mine, and it was a common practice to conduct external searches among the limited talent pool of former or current CEOs. Nevertheless, the board was unanimous in its decision. The board believed it was time to shake things up in the Company and that I was the one to do it. So I assumed the reins and began a journey unlike anything I could have ever foreseen.

Less than a month after assuming the role as the Company's figurehead, an incident involving employee misconduct in the workspace became known throughout the organization. An inner-office romance had escalated out of control. Several employees witnessed "inappropriate conduct"—to put it mildly—in the workplace and reported it. Just a few weeks later, several employees got drunk at the annual company picnic at a private swim club and had gone skinny-dipping after most people, including me, had gone home. The situation had gotten so out of hand the police were called and several employees—including a number of senior managers—were arrested. The story made local headlines. I didn't think things could get any worse, but I was wrong. A month later, I received a call from a regional director informing me that three members of management had been terminated for abusive treatment of subordinates, lack of confidence, and failures in their ability to lead. Allegations surfaced that some employees were padding their expense reports and that others were conducting personal business on company time. Some were alleged to have disclosed confidential client information to their colleagues as a part of routine discussion. The Company, it seemed, was falling apart at the seams.

I had never been a quitter, but I realized as the central figure of the Company, responsibility for the recent debacles fell on my shoulders, and it wouldn't be long until the board asked for my resignation or terminated me. I wrote my resignation and saved the file on my computer. After lunch, I'd print it, sign it, and send it to the chairwoman of the board. On a whim, I decided to grab lunch at a local deli. It had become a favorite haunt of mine when I had time for a quick bite. I arrived, placed my order, and waited in front of the deli counter. I planned to take my sandwich back to the office and eat in silence. While looking at the different lunch meats in the case, I heard a voice.

"Cheryl? Cheryl Stevens?"

I turned and looked in the direction of the familiar voice. "Rob? Robert Clark! My goodness, how long has it been?"

He gave me a big hug. "Since grad school. Eight, ten years, I guess," he said as he thought about it. "What are you up to these days?" he asked.

I was ready to blurt out my title, but then I recalled the recent headlines and scandals and simply said, "I'm with the Company."

"Yeah, I saw your name in the paper," he said as though offering his condolences. I blushed, genuinely embarrassed. Just as I opened my mouth to say something, he said, "Listen, I'm glad I ran into you. I know someone who can help you." He reached into his pocket and produced a business card, which he handed to me. "He's a friend of mine. Really good. He helped my company a few years ago. Give him a call, and tell him I referred you."

I was about to protest when he heard his order called and said, "Cheryl, that's me. I have to go. It was great to see you again. Call that number, and let me know how you make out." And with that, he was gone.

I looked down at the unassuming card. It simply said, "The Consultant" and contained the standard contact information. I placed it in my pocket, waited for my sandwich, and eventually headed back to the office to place a call that would change my life.

A few days after my initial phone call, the Consultant arrived and met with me. I provided him with the details of some of the recent debacles. He listened attentively, nodding from time to time. When I had finished, and sensing my exasperation, he informed me that he could indeed help. He outlined a plan, requested unlimited access to my employees, and told me he could get started right away.

At my wit's end, I consented. With that, the Consultant shot up out of his chair and was gone. I sent an e-mail to all employees, apprising them of the Consultant's presence and asked everyone to be cooperative and forthright. The next day, he arrived very early. I noticed him sitting in his car when I pulled into my reserved spot in front of the building. He just sat there taking notes. I smiled at him, and he gave me a friendly wave. I wasn't sure what to make of him. I trusted Robert's judgment, but I had to admit his behavior seemed a bit strange for a consultant.

For several weeks, I observed the Consultant milling about, talking to employees. Seemingly, he was around every corner I turned. One day, he arrived in khakis and a polo shirt. He smiled as he greeted me and headed straight for the loading dock, where he spent the entire morning. Later that same day, I received word he was in the shipping department helping load packages while talking with the employees about their plans for the upcoming holiday. He was talking about sports, news, and joking around with everyone. Another day, he was in the break room having coffee and doughnuts, which he provided, with members of the receptionist pool as well as a few account executives. He talked about their families, children, school, and what they had done over the weekend. He navigated the maze of cubicles on a daily basis like a skilled lab rat and chatted with everyone. After a few weeks, he had become a familiar face and was greeting everyone by name. Employees had really taken a shine to him and would freely engage him in conversation.

One day, he sat in the chair opposite my desk and when asked about his progress, responded with a question, "Cheryl, what are the Company's core values?" I was silent. I hadn't expected a question. Mentally, I groped for the answer. A small laugh escaped from my lips as I said, "What do they have to do with the Company's current situation?" The Consultant remained silent, and it became clear he was not going to speak until I answered his question.

Finally I began, "Well…our core values involve respecting others, our clients, and—"

He cut me off. "Please simply state what they are."

I stammered, "I…I…I can't recall them verbatim right now, but…,"

"You're in good company, Cheryl. Neither can most of your employees." He then stated, "Integrity, loyalty, and service."

"What?" I asked, a bit confused.

"Integrity, loyalty, and service. Those are the Company's core values," he said. "Cheryl, the time I spent with your employees, the assessment I conducted, and the survey I utilized revealed the company's culture is not in alignment with its professed values." He paused. "This is a serious issue for you, because values are the currency of leadership." He then presented me with his consulting report, which I scrutinized.

Cheryl Stevens
The Company
Dear Miss Stevens:

Thank you for choosing my firm to address your organization's leadership needs. I am delighted to serve you. As requested, my consulting report is attached. In it you will find my analysis and observations of your recent Organizational Cultural Assessment. My analysis was compiled based on the Organizational Cultural Assessment Instrument (OCAI), which rates six key dimensions of organizational culture. Additionally, the report contains a summary of personal interviews and survey responses.

This report outlines the findings of the OCAI, interviews, and a values survey and provides the following:

- Analysis of OCAI findings
- Analysis of interview data
- Survey responses
- Review strengths and weaknesses
- Recommend improvements to increase efficiency and accuracy

Please contact me if you have any questions or if I can be of further service. Thank you again for allowing me to serve you!

Sincerely,
The Consultant

Executive Summary

This report covers the findings, analysis, and current research on organizational culture at The Company. It provides detailed information on the type of culture within the organization as well as identifies the preferred, or future, culture. Key findings of this report are:

- Current culture favors the Market style
- A competing Hierarchy style
- Preferred culture that favors the Clan style
- Perception of favoritism
- Lack of awareness and relevance of company values

An analysis of the OCAI findings revealed The Company functions as a market. That is, it is primarily concerned with the external environment. This is particularly relevant given the mission of The Company to support its customers and provide superior customer service. Personal interviews and a values survey revealed a lack of awareness and regard for Company values. The following recommendations are made:

- Institute an effective employee survey program for systematically monitoring employee attitudes and ideas.
- Conduct internal assessment to ascertain the real issues.

- Implement interactive corporate values training program.
- Increase the effectiveness of the employee suggestion box.
- Energize the employee recognition system.

Incorporating these recommendations will allow The Company to progress toward the preferred culture, Clan. This promotes collaboration, teamwork, and unity and fosters an atmosphere of trust and loyalty. It will create awareness and ownership of company values and increase ethical behavior.

After reading the executive summary, I flipped through the report itself in which the results of his observations and analysis were detailed. I was a bit surprised by what I read. Having been with the Company for a number of years, I thought I knew its culture, people, and values. What I read gave me serious doubts about what I actually knew.

I discussed the report at length with the Consultant and expressed my concern. He grew silent and hesitated before he spoke, choosing his words carefully. "Cheryl," he said evenly, "there's an issue I thought best to leave out of my report. However, it's something we need to discuss because it could have a significant impact on you and the Company."

"What is it?" I asked, genuinely concerned.

"Well," he began, "you're the first female CEO in the company's history. You're somewhat junior in comparison to the other VPs and were selected ahead of them—"

"Wait a minute!" I cut him off sharply, leaning forward in my chair, my voice rising. "Are you suggesting that I used promiscuous means to obtain my current position?"

"I'm not suggesting that at all, Cheryl."

"Then why…,"

"Your people are," he deadpanned. "At least, that is a common perception."

I sat back in my chair, stunned. I didn't know what to say. Surely it couldn't be many people who thought that way. I leaned forward again. "It can't be that many people who think that. Some people are just antiquated in the way they think. They can't handle having a female CEO, so they spread rumors and make up stories to justify their perceptions."

He sat motionless. The blank look on his face gave away the truth.

"It's not just a few people who believe that, is it?" I asked.

"No. I'm afraid not," was all he said.

Wow! The report indicated we had problems, but I had no idea things were this bad. After pondering this for a few minutes, I finally said, "I had no idea people thought that about me. I'm really shocked."

"I can see that," he said. "It's not as if anyone is going to tell you, Cheryl."

"I know," I said dejectedly, "but the thought never occurred to me." I paused in contemplation. "Okay, what do you suggest I do?"

He referred me to the recommendations section of the report. I skimmed through them, stopping occasionally to ask questions. We had a lengthy discussion about what he thought I should do. When we were finished, I asked the Consultant if he would assist with the implementation of his recommendations. He agreed. His recommendations consisted of an in-depth training program for all employees that would eventually become known at the Company as the Leadership Academy, a five-day, interactive seminar designed to educate, challenge, and unite all employees—including me, the board of directors, and all senior executives.

DAY 1
DEFINING VALUES

*If we are to go forward, we must go back
and rediscover those precious values—that
all reality hinges on moral foundations
and that all reality has spiritual control.*

—Martin Luther King, Jr.

Agenda

On the first day of the Leadership Academy, I stood by the door to the Company's training room. I anticipated greeting the members of the board and senior management, whom I assumed would be the first to attend the training. I was genuinely surprised when some junior staff members arrived in addition to just a few members of the board and upper management. I looked to the Consultant for help, but he simply smiled and extended the same warm greeting to everyone. *Okay,* I thought, *this must be some sort of attempt to level the playing field. I'll just go with it and explain to the board members later.*

I recalled that the Consultant's report indicated the training sessions would include a diverse representation of personnel, but I didn't think he would include the board members and senior managers with everyone. The group was limited to thirty people—five per table, and they were numbered—and once everyone had taken their seats, I mounted the podium and made some brief introductory remarks before turning things over to the Consultant. I took my seat at the assigned table.

The Consultant smiled warmly again, welcomed everyone, and reviewed the agenda for the week. "This program is designed to be interactive. On your tables, you will find a packet that contains a syllabus, daily schedule for the week, small group assignments, case studies, and relevant information for group discussions." He opened his copy of the packet and reviewed the material. "This morning, we will begin with a discussion about values, and then break into small groups. Please see your assignment sheet for your group's meeting location."

My group consisted of the receptionist, facilities manager, account executive, and shipping clerk, and our assigned small group location was in conference room one. "This afternoon, we will meet back here for another discussion, followed by a small group discussion, then a large group discussion, and end-of-day wrap-up with breaks in between. Each small group member will get a chance to lead the group. Group leaders, please see me for instructions prior to each small group meeting. I will review the purpose of the small group discussion and provide directions to each small group leader prior to the discussion. On your table, you will find class climate assessments (figure 1.) These are to be completed daily, preferably by a different person each day. I'll review them with the class the following day. In your student packets, there is an end-of-course critique that is broken down by day and topic. I recommend you fill it out daily while the material is fresh in your mind. Also in your packet are directions for your group presentation, which will be held at the end of class on Friday. Look those over and discuss them with your small group members. Does anyone have any questions?" No one did.

Training Feedback From   Day: _____

Please circle a number that describes your feelings about the following. The higher the number circles, the more satisfied you felt.

1. Overall value of the training.

1 2 3 4 5 6 7 8 9 10

Comments: _____

_____

2. Was the training easy to follow:

1 2 3 4 5 6 7 8 9 10

Comments: _____

_____

3. Will you be able to use the knowledge in your job?

1 2 3 4 5 6 7 8 9 10

Comments: _____

_____

4. How would you rate the instructor?

1 2 3 4 5 6 7 8 9 10

Comments: _____

_____

General comments or suggestions.

_____

_____

_____

Figure 1

Values

He surveyed the room quickly and said, "Beginning with table one, I would like everyone to count off from one to six." When we had finished counting, he instructed everyone to relocate to the table that corresponded to their individual number. All of the ones were at table one and so forth. This definitely mixed things up. All of the executives and upper management had been at one table, and the other tables had been made up of peer groups. When we had settled at our new table, the Consultant instructed us introduce ourselves to one another, fill out the blank name placard in our packet, and indicate the number of years we had been with the Company. After we finished, took turns standing at a table, and introduced the person to our right using the provided introduction sheet as a guide, which identified the hometown, family status, hobbies, position with the Company, and years of service. As we did, the Consultant kept track of the cumulative number of years with the Company—112 in total for the group—and wrote it on the whiteboard.

He said, "We have over one-hundred years of Company experience in this room, so I'm sure we will have some terrific conversations this week." He displayed a Power Point slide on the screen in the front of the room.

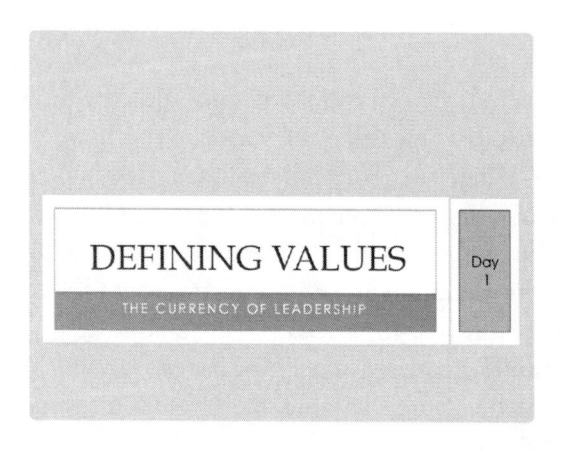

> **DEFINING VALUES**
> THE CURRENCY OF LEADERSHIP
>
> Day 1

He continued, "During the past several weeks, I have spoken with and met all of the Company's employees, including the chief executive officer and members of the board—some of whom are here today." He smiled as he looked at the board members present. "We discussed a variety of subjects and concerns about the Company, as many of you will recall. I implemented several tools to assess the Company's culture and core value awareness. Additionally, I made observations regarding the Company's daily business practices, professionalism, personal relationships, and politics." He paused as he began to slowly walk around the room. "Many of the people with whom I spoke, expressed concern for the lack of leadership they observed in the Company." *Oh, great,* I thought. *I might as well have a bull's eye on my back.* "Leadership is an expansive term and means different things to different people; and while it may be difficult to define and articulate, what we are going examine this week is what I like to call the *currency of leadership*. That is, the various components that comprise leadership and make it effective—or not, for that matter," he added as an afterthought. "Much like actual currency, leadership is comprised of various denominations that together give it value and worth. Today, we are going to discuss values and the role they play in leadership. Each day, we will discuss a different topic or denomination that relates to leadership."

He stood by a chart and flipped the cover sheet over the top. Underneath was a sheet he had previously filled out with the Company's core values, *integrity, loyalty,* and *service*. "Since the topic of the day is values, let's begin by identifying the Company's core values," he said, motioning to the chart. He tore the top sheet off and hung it on the wall. "Let's add to this list," he said, picking up a marker. "Someone give me a value." Members of the group called out values, which the Consultant wrote on the chart.

responsibility	commitment	integrity
respect for others	purpose	loyalty
truth	caring	patience
honesty	positivity	trust
transparency	accountability	stewardship
innovation	openness	courtesy
equality	quality	efficiency
compassion	teamwork	consistency

"Great," he said as he tore the page and hung it on the wall. "These are going to our class values and norms, the rules by which we will abide for the week." After he posted the page, he instructed us to discuss them as a table and choose the one we believed was the most important and write in on the sign provided. We chose one and wrote it on the large t-stand sign in the center of the table. My table chose integrity as our value. The other tables chose trust, honesty, compassion, loyalty, and respect. We were now known by our table name, not our table number.

The Consultant began. "Okay," he said. "Several weeks ago you should have received an e-mail link to a survey. Did everyone receive that and complete it?" Everyone nodded. "We all have values, beliefs about life, right and wrong, and proper behavior. It's not a stretch to state that all people have a basic concept of right and wrong as it pertains to their overall interaction with one another within the confines of society. Of course, depending on the society and its culture, there may be variations. Nevertheless, a set of values is present and can be observed." He referred us to our student packet, which contained a list of definitions. "In general," he said, "values are socially and personally shared conceptions of the good, desirable, and righteous. They are stabilized beliefs about personally or socially preferred modes of conduct or end-states of existence. They determine how one ought to or ought not to behave or act.[5] In conversations, we qualify values using words like *ought*, *should*, *good*, *right*, and *fair*. Furthermore, a value is an enduring belief that a specific mode of conduct or end-state of existence is personally or socially preferable to an opposite or converse mode of conduct or end-state of existence."[6]

He picked up a remote from the podium and pointed it at the large screen behind him as he stepped aside. Instantly, a slide appeared. "Let's take a look at some definitions of values. Would someone from table honesty please read this?"

A board member at the table read its contents.

> **VALUES DEFINITIONS**
>
> - A concept of the desirable, which influences the selection from available modes, means, and ends of action.
>
> - An enduring belief that a specific mode of conduct or end-state of existence is personally or socially preferable to an opposite or converse mode of conduct or end-state of existence.
>
> - Concepts or beliefs pertaining to desirable end-states or behaviors, transcending specific situations, guiding selection or evaluation of behaviors and events, and ordered by relative importance.
>
> - Desirable trans-situational goal, varying in importance that serves as a guiding principal in the life of a person or other social entity.
>
> Kloyula, Nina. *Basic Human Values in the Workplace*. (2008). 6. (accessed June 30, 2014).

"Thank you," he said, beginning to move around the room. "Values are so central to an individual's personality and cognitive structure that they influence every facet of human behavior—attitudes, decisions, moral judgments, evaluations, and social action. Intrinsic qualities of values determine our outer behavior. People seek these qualities in activities they engage, in objects they acquire, in principles they cultivate, in situations they live through, in professions they work, and in evaluations they make. Values are, thus, prime drivers of personal, social, and professional choices. Here are some of your definitions from the survey you completed." He advanced the slide. I saw a few people smile as they recognized their definitions.

> ### SURVEY DEFINITIONS
>
> - A person's moral compass that determines right and wrong.
> - Beliefs that influence behavior.
> - The principles that one uses to make decisions and develop priorities.
> - Values are a set of guidelines that provide guidance to what is good, bad, normal, etc.

"Let's build on these," he said as he slowly moved about the room. "Who can add to this?"

A young girl from table four said, "In a general sense, values are beliefs that one holds to be true, right, and moral. They provide a method from distinguishing right from wrong, in both an individual and collective sense. More importantly, they serve as a personal guide for behavior and conduct."

"Excellent!" he said. "Indeed, every person needs a well-thought-out philosophy of life to provide direction and give meaning to life. At the core of a philosophy of life is a set of values, a set of basic beliefs that defines what a person stands for.[7] Values serve as a standard against which we evaluate situations. When we evaluate something, we compare it to a standard. We determine whether it meets that standard or falls short, comes close or far exceeds. To evaluate is to determine the merit of a thing or an action as compared to a standard."[8] He paused as he surveyed the room before continuing. "The implication is values are in some abstract or remote way good by nature, and are an intrinsic quality present in all human beings that provides moral direction. If this were universally true, immoral behavior would not exist—or at least, not to the expansive extent present in society today. And if this were universally true, we might not be having this training." He smiled and let his words sink in. "Values have three components," he stated holding up three fingers and advancing the slide. "Would someone from table respect read these, please?"

> ## THREE COMPONENTS
>
> 1. Cognition about the desirable
>
> 2. Affective in the sense one can be emotional about it
>
> 3. A behavioral component in that it can be translated into action.
>
> Rokeach, Milton, The Nature of Human Values, Accessed June 27, 2014, 5.

"Thank you. What does it mean values are cognitive?"

"It means to give them thought or think about them," a man from the adjacent table said.

"Yes, values require thought. What else?"

"They have an intellectual component," a woman chimed in.

"Great! Why are we emotional about our values?"

"Because they define who we are and what we believe."

"Absolutely," he said. "But why do we get emotional about them?"

"Not everyone has the same values, and we get defensive when what we believe is challenged," I said.

"Terrific!" he said. "Tell me, do you get emotional about your values because they are being challenged or because you can't defend them as well as you'd like?"

"Probably a little bit of both," I mused.

He smiled. "Sure. We don't like it when we're backed into a corner, right? So how do values influence our behavior?"

"We behave based on what we believe," a man at table loyalty stated. "Our values guide our behavior."

"Yes!" The Consultant said excitedly. "Exactly. Our values govern our behavior and guide us." He became very animated as he moved around the room frenetically.

"Do you believe they apply equally to men and women?" Everyone agreed they did. He continued, "You're right, they do," he said. "However, values differ among men and women. Men ascribe more importance to power, achievement, stimulation, hedonism, and self-direction; and women ascribed more importance to universalism and benevolence.[9] Nevertheless, values are central to who we are, what we think, and how we act on a daily basis. They affect every aspect of our lives.

In fact, values are so deep-seated that one never actually *sees* values themselves. What is seen are the ways through which values manifest themselves (e.g., in opinions, attitudes, preferences, desires, fears, etc.) Values can be personal, professional, organizational, or societal. Although they are interrelated, the influence among them varies."[10]

One of the members of table honesty raised his hand and asked, "So values determine who we are, right?"

The Consultant was quite exuberant when he replied. "Yes! Absolutely. Values epitomize what we believe and give credence to our opinions. They provide the substance of our discussions and arguments. We are both defined by them and governed by them. The essence of who we are is contained within the confines of our values. No other singular element so accurately and explicitly personifies us. Think about this…,"—he paused for effect—"some of the more important and more universally accepted values are integrity, respect, loyalty, and responsibility.[11] These values correspond to the values you identified as important to you," he said, pointing to the list on the wall. Many heads were nodding, including mine. I had listed integrity at the top of my list.

An older gentleman from table trust, spoke, "I disagree that values influence our behavior. I think values play a part in how we act, but how we act depends on the situation. It's like trying to decide which came first, the chicken or the egg. Do values shape us or do we shape our values?"

The Consultant redirected his question and asked the group what they thought. What a way to incite conversation! Many started speaking at the same time, and some tried to talk over each other. It became evident there was disparity in the group.

"Values determine how we act!" one woman said. "The situation doesn't matter."

"No, the situation is going determine which values we tap into. It does matter."

"Our values control our behavior, not the other way around."

"Uh-uh, not true. I control my values and what I believe and how I will act."

The debate continued for several minutes. Finally, the Consultant said, "Okay, everyone, this is a great discussion, and it will provide a good foundation for your first small group discussion."

I checked my watch. Our morning session had gone quickly. The Consultant began to introduce the topic of our first small group discussion. "As you will discuss in your small groups, research is divided about whether values develop naturally, based on individual personality and external influence, or if they are in fact selected by an individual in order to justify behavior and satisfy desires, as evidenced by the previous discussion. This rationalization demonstrates the cognitive component of value development and substantiates the existence of a selection process. For example, 'I believe that X is good because believing so serves my psychological interests.'[12] In other words, we choose our values based on our desires, not some innate moral component. This perspective explains the variation in values that manifests itself in socially inappropriate behavior. If you recall, one of the survey questions asked, Do you adopt values that justify your behavior? The majority of you said no. This indicates most of you believe values are a constant and your behavior is reflection of that constant. Additional survey responses revealed the majority of you believe your actions align with your values, and you do not adopt values that justify your behavior. Essentially, you behavior is a reflection of your values and not the inverse. These results do not negate the possibility that values are chosen based on psychological interests. As you will discuss, research suggests people who pursue intrinsic values report higher levels of self-actualization and show higher overall global functioning.[13] Perhaps value development is a reflection of personality in conjunction with pursuing those things that provide a positive psychological experience that leads to personal harmony and balance within the social construct."

He returned to the podium and glanced at the syllabus. "Okay, we're going to break into our small groups. I need this morning's group leaders to remain here while everyone takes this opportunity to grab some coffee, use the bathroom, and stretch your legs."

Fittingly, I suppose, I was assigned as the leader of the morning group. The other group leaders and I sat at the front table and awaited our assignment. "Okay," the Consultant said to the group leaders who stayed behind, "While values define us and represent our most cherished beliefs, the question your group must answer, before we proceed with a detailed analysis of values and their relationship to leadership, is: *Where do values originate?*"

He handed each of us a folder and instructed us to review the contents before proceeding to our small group.

Once there, we were to facilitate a discussion that attempted to answer the assigned question and be prepared to discuss our findings with the main group on Friday.

In the Beginning

I entered the conference room and found everyone seated around the table. Part of the small group requirement, as outlined in the instructions and reviewed by the Consultant, was for everyone to introduce him or herself. Unlike my random table assignment for the large group, The Consultant had carefully selected the small groups prior to the training. When I arrived, members of my group were still discussing whether values influenced our behavior or if behavior influenced our values. I interrupted, quickly introduced myself, and listed integrity as my value. When everyone had finished, I consulted the instructions before proceeding.

"Okay," I said, reading from the folder, "Many people believe we are born with a set of basic values that are somewhat fixed during childhood and become more fluid and susceptible to change during adolescence and early adulthood. According to the survey we took, we are pretty much evenly split with those who believed individuals were born with an internal moral compass, just slightly edging out those who believed the opposite." I paused for a moment and glanced at my group members. "Does everyone agree?" I asked. Everyone nodded except for the receptionist. She said, "I believe we are born with the potential to develop values but not with values, if you know what I mean." I nodded and said, "Yes, I know what you mean."

The account executive chimed in, "I kind of agree, because if we were born with values, wouldn't we all have similar values?"

"I think we are born with basic values, but they change over time based on a variety of things such as family, friends, environment, etc.," the facilities manager said.

I nodded, looked down at the folder, and continued, "Well," I began, "research data suggests the mental fiber necessary for value formation is present in children and begins to form in the latter years of development. One scholar noted that children focus on concrete, observable elements of their world, but they also begin to organize these elements into trait categories when they describe themselves and other persons.[14] In other words, I guess what they are trying to say is that as children get older, enter adolescence, and later adulthood, they become cognizant of their interaction with their environment and begin to identify what's important to them." I looked up. The Consultant noted group leaders were to check for understanding frequently and solicit input from the group by asking questions, some of which were provided in the folder. "That makes sense to me. Does anyone have a different opinion?"

The facilities manager reiterated, "I think people are influenced by others—family, friends, peers—and as a result, develop a set of values they carry with them throughout their lives. This is probably what leads to prioritization and the establishment of values based on their personality and environmental influence."

The account manager said, "Your perspective presupposes that the necessary elements for the formation of values are innate to everyone, and that they're an intrinsic characteristic that's part of our DNA makeup."

"I suppose," he said. "But most people with a common culture, or at least a common foundation, seem to have similar values."

I was a bit surprised; we were actually having an interesting discussion. I consulted the folder and chimed in, "It says here, research suggests values possess both a collective and individual element that 'values arise in experiences of self-formation and self-transcendence.'[15] What do you think about that?"

This time, it was the shipping clerk who spoke up. "So, essentially, you're saying we pick and choose our values based on who we are and how we interact with our environment, right?"

"Well, I'm not saying that, the research is, I think. However, it seems values are determined by such factors as family upbringing, religious beliefs, social and cultural influence, convenience, and need." I pulled five copies of a handout from the folder and passed them around the table. On it were listed ten basic motivators for the establishment of values that existed in a circular continuum. I informed the group we were to pick the motivator with which we most closely identified.

1. *Conformity*: Restraint of actions, inclinations, and impulses likely to upset or harm others and violate social expectations or norms.
2. *Tradition*: Respect, commitment, and acceptance of the customs and ideas that one's culture or religion provides.
3. *Benevolence*: Caring for the welfare of the people with whom one is in frequent personal contact.
4. *Universalism*: Understanding, appreciation, tolerance, and protection for the welfare of all people and nature.
5. *Self-direction*: Independent thought and action—choosing, creating, exploring.
6. *Stimulation*: Excitement, novelty, and challenge in life.
7. *Hedonism*: Pleasure, gratification of the senses.
8. *Achievement*: Personal success through demonstrating competence in accordance with social standards.
9. *Power*: Social status and prestige, control and dominance over people and resources.
10. *Security*: Safety, harmony, and stability of society, of relationships, and of self.[16]

We were divided in our choices. The account executive chose *power*. *That's quite fitting*, I thought. The shipping clerk chose *security*. *That seems to match your personality*, I mused to myself. The receptionist chose *benevolence*. She seemed like the charitable type. The facilities manager chose *universalism*. *Interesting*, I thought. He seemed more likely to choose power to me. I chose *self-direction* because I was raised to be independent and not rely on others.

As I reviewed the handout, I glanced at the other items in the folder. One of the documents contained Maslow's Hierarchy of Needs (figure 2), which I shared with the group. At the top was a question, which I read aloud. "Do needs lead to the development of values?"

Everyone began to talk at once, and two discussions broke out. I ran my finger down the page hoping to find something to bring everyone back to a common theme. "Okay," I said reading from the file. "Some researchers reject the idea that values are associated with needs, citing that animals have needs yet have no values. Let me read this quote:

'Man is the only animal that can be meaningfully described as having values. Values are the cognitive representations and transformation of needs, and man is the only animal capable of such representations and transformations of needs.'[17]"

In other words," the account executive asked, "needs alone is not the singular basis for value development, right?"

"Yes," I said. "They arise from a cognitive understanding of a need that lies beyond mere instinct. However, it is imperative to understand how needs factor into value development within the cognitive process."

"So values are based on needs that have been thought about?" the shipping clerk asked.

"Something like that, yes," I said.

"So you're telling me I have to think about being hungry in order to value food?" asked the facilities manager condescendingly.

"That's not what it means," the account executive said. "It simply means that we think about our actions, which is based on what we believe in—our values."

"I don't think about eating when I'm hungry," the facilities manager said.

"So you just eat whatever you see, you don't read the menu?" asked the account executive.

He thought for a moment. "Okay, I can see your point, but I just don't think it's that cut and dry."

"Agreed," he said.

I glanced down at the folder again. Leading this discussion was no joke. As I skimmed along the instructions, I said, "Okay, according to this information, Maslow's Hierarchy of needs identifies three universal requirements into which everyone is born. They are:

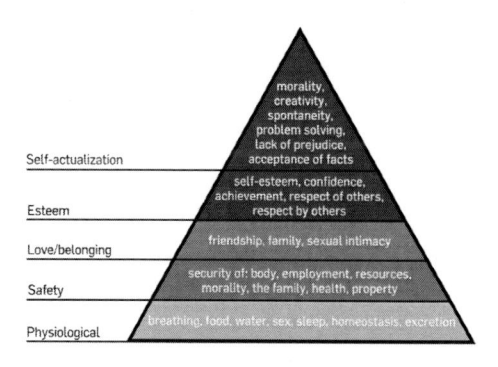

```
                          morality,
                         creativity,
                        spontaneity,
                       problem solving,
                      lack of prejudice,
Self-actualization   acceptance of facts
                    self-esteem, confidence,
                  achievement, respect of others,
Esteem              respect by others
                 friendship, family, sexual intimacy
Love/belonging
               security of: body, employment, resources,
Safety           morality, the family, health, property
              breathing, food, water, sex, sleep, homeostasis, excretion
Physiological
```

1. Needs of the individual as a biological organism.
2. Requisites of coordinated social interaction.
3. Needs of groups for survival and welfare."[18]

The facilities manager piped in, "According to what I see here on this chart, these requirements range from basic survival to social and emotional development, right? And external factors such as environment and culture combine with these requirements and lead to the formation of values. Is that how everyone else sees it?"

Everyone remained silent as they studied the chart. Finally, I said, "Well, it seems we are in agreement that external factors combine with the requirements and lead to the formation of values."

"So that's it?" the shipping clerk asked. "We form values based on our needs?"

"I see it as our needs determining our values," the receptionist said.

"Me too," said the facilities manager.

"That might be true in an arbitrary sense," the account executive said. "But our needs change based on our situation. We aren't living in caves and hunting our food. We can just run to the store, so our value for food is going to be different than primitive man's, not to mention, the abundance of the food supply today."

"True," shot in the facilities manager. "But we all have needs, and those needs will affect our values."

"Yes," I agreed. "Once our lower-order needs are met, we will pursue higher-order needs. However, all of our needs, whatever they are at the time, will affect our values."

I thumbed through the folder and looked for the next topic of discussion. I came across the last page of the small group instructions. I pulled the page from the folder, skimmed it, and then read the pertinent information.

"This states there are four value domains that can be directly attributed to Maslow's Hierarchy of Needs, and that they are direct contributors to value development." I read them aloud one at a time.

1. The *security domain* of values incorporates the basic need to physically survive. This domain is directly related to Maslow's physiological needs that say individuals seek out basic human needs required to sustain life, which include food, clothing, and shelter.

2. The *achievement domain* of values consists of the development and utilization of skills from available resources in the physical and social environment. This domain is directly related to Maslow's need for self-esteem, where the individual desires more personal recognition and recognition from others through achievements that produce self-confidence, prestige, power, and control.
3. The *prosocial domain* of values encompasses the concern for the well being of others. This domain is directly related to Maslow's need for affiliation, which states that individuals desire to belong to and be accepted by various social groups.
4. The *maturity domain* of values is comprised of attaining goals through life experiences, learning, and understanding to appreciate social and physical reality. This domain relates directly to Maslow's need for self-actualization, which says individuals have a need to maximize one's potential and to become what one is capable of becoming.[19]

We all contemplated the information for a moment. The account executive was the first to speak. "These domains suggest the necessary 'material' for the formation of values is inherent to all of us, and that the domains build upon one another and act in tandem within individual's needs and ultimately, form one's values. That's how I take it."

"Me too," said the receptionist. "What we've studied seems to suggest value development is a process that originates with the basic need and cognitive understanding of sustenance and later evolves into the mature phase of learning and goal attainment."

"I agree," I said. "However, the formation of individual values throughout the process is not without influence." I glanced at the document. "One researcher made five assumptions about values that coincide with the domain theory that is pretty interesting.

1. The total number of values that a person possesses is relatively small.
2. All men everywhere possess the same values to different degrees.
3. Values are organized into values systems.
4. The antecedents of human values can be traced to culture, society and its institutions, and personality.
5. The consequences of human values will be manifested in virtually all phenomena that social scientists might consider worth investigating and understanding."[20]

Everyone nodded in contemplative silence. It was time to wrap-up the small group discussion and go to lunch.

We concluded that in essence values govern our daily lives, the decisions we make, the way we interact with others, the careers we choose, the friends we make, the relationships we develop, what we eat, where we live, and what we believe. 'The function of human values is to satisfy needs and at the same time to maintain self-esteem.'[21]

We also noted that values are perpetually evolving from the time we are born. They are externally influenced by our environment and culture, which plays a significant role in value development with regard to the four value domains. We develop values in childhood and early adolescence that are subject to change when we enter adulthood. In adulthood, there are three causes of value change: a historical event that has an impact on specific age cohorts (e.g., war, depression); physical aging (e.g., loss of strength); and life stage (e.g., child bearing age, widowhood).[22]

It is these changes, or a combination of them, that causes our values to evolve over time and settle in a somewhat fixed manner later in life. However, this does not negate the possibility of further change, which can occur based on cultural and environmental factors. We were going to discuss this issue as a large group after lunch.

A Matter of Culture

After lunch, we all filtered back into the training room. I had to admit, I enjoyed the morning session. What's more, I was engaged in discussion with members of my group after our meeting and ended up having lunch with them in the employee cafeteria. I normally would have had lunch in my office or in the executive lunchroom. Instead, I found myself caught up in a lively discussion with my employees about their values and the Company's values.

The Consultant asked how our morning small group had gone. Everyone said it had gone well, and he seemed genuinely pleased. "Let's take a moment and review some of what you discussed," he said. We spent about ten minutes discussing the origin of values. It was clear the Consultant wanted us to have a firm understanding of how our values develop and the role they play in our daily lives.

He introduced the afternoon's topics, *culture* and *values*. He began, "Now that we have defined values, identified those values most important to us, and are clear on their origin, we are going to look at the effect culture has on value formation and on our actions. Does the Company have a culture?" Just about everyone nodded.

"Yes, you're correct. Organizations have their own, unique cultures. The Company is no different, as we shall see." He walked over and stood next to the chart and said, "Describe the Company's culture for me in just a few words."

"Competitive," one person shouted out.

"Rewarding," said another.

"Cutthroat."

"Privileged."

"Corrupt." *Corrupt? Really?* I was genuinely shocked someone would say the Company's culture was corrupt. The Consultant didn't bat an eye and continued to write.

"Abrasive." It seemed the culture was devolving now after the "corrupt" comment.

"Ethically challenged." *Oh, great,* I thought. *Let's just keep piling in on!*

"Okay," he said at last. "We have a pretty good list here. Is anyone surprised by these responses?"

I raised my hand. "Frankly, I am. I wouldn't characterize our culture as corrupt."

"Okay," he said. "Let's explore that." He turned to the woman who made the comment. "So why do you believe the culture is corrupt?"

She was a little embarrassed about being put on the spot, but she responded, "Well, I've been here for a few years, and I've noticed some people pad their expense reports. They exaggerate the amount of miles they travel. Some claim they are leaving for a business meeting and go home for the day or run personal errands on company time."

What! I thought. My expression must have betrayed my thoughts. The Consultant looked right at me. "Are you sure about that?" I asked.

She nodded. "Yes. I don't want to name names, but a certain individual said she was attending a business meeting one day, and when I went out for lunch, I saw her getting her nails done."

"I see," was all I could manage to say.

The Consultant said, "Okay. Let's discuss that in terms of organizational culture. Do think that individual did that because she believed it was acceptable?"

"I guess she figured it wasn't really a big deal. Yes."

"Do you believe that is part of the Company's culture?" he asked.

I wanted to answer, but I refrained and allowed her to answer. "I don't know," she hesitated. "I suppose."

"Interesting," he said. "Organizations are often a mix of competing cultures. If you recall, I conducted a survey in which I asked everyone to assess the culture of the organization." She nodded as he spoke. "The survey I used was the Organizational Culture Assessment Instrument (OCAI), which was developed by Kim Cameron and Robert Quinn. They developed the model of the Competing Values Framework, which consists of four Competing Values that correspond with four types of organizational culture."[23] He paused as he surveyed the room. "Every organization has its own mix of these four types of organizational culture. This mix is found by the completion of a short questionnaire, which you all took."[24]

He presented a slide with a diagram.

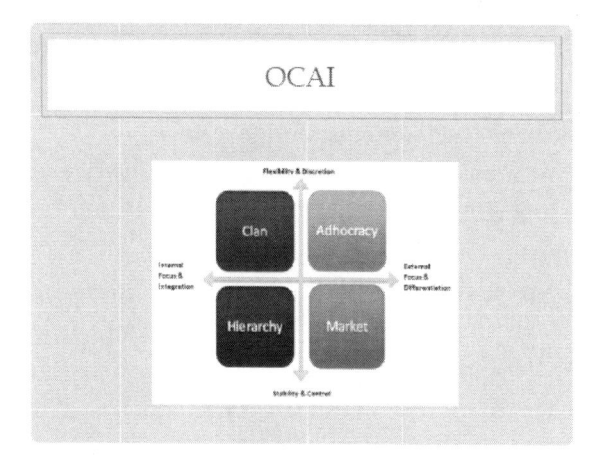

"This represents an Organizational Culture Assessment Instrument (OCAI), which assesses six dimensions of organizational culture. The Company has a market culture. Market organizations are characterized by competitiveness and productivity, which is conducive to success in an organization that is based on serving the needs of their customers. Due to the nature of the Company's business, it is not surprising that the OCAI revealed a results-driven work environment. In a business where the stakes are high, the market culture emphasizes winning amidst competitive actions and goal completion.[25] The OCAI revealed the preferred culture was a *clan*. That is, employees would like to work in a collaborative environment. Clan cultures are based on a high level of teamwork and a friendly work environment akin to a big family. They thrive on loyalty and trust and promote the expression of opinions and ideas, which is consistent with the values you identified this morning. Often, such organizations have a high commitment level amongst employees."

Well, I thought, *that is certainly true around here. Everything revolved around success, but I always considered the Company to be a team.*

He continued, "Culture is a collective term in that it involves the sharing of ideas, beliefs, and values. It is forged through common experiences, history, and language. 'Language reinforces cultural norms and has a unifying effect within a single geographic border. On a global scale, it serves the purpose of distinguishing nations and cultures from one another.'[26] Essentially, culture is what makes Americans American and Chinese Chinese. It is that intangible quality that defines a group of people within the social construct."

He showed another slide and asked a member of table loyalty to read it.

> **CULTURE**
>
> Culture is defined a distinctive normative systems consisting of model patterns of shared psychological properties among member of collectivities that result in compelling common affective, attitudinal, and behavioral orientations that are transmitted across generations and that differentiate collectivities from each other.
>
> Robert House, Norman Wright, and Ram Aditya. "Cross-Cultural Research on Organizational Leadership: A Critical Analysis and a Proposed Theory," in New Perspectives on International Industrial/Organizational Psychology ed. P. Christopher Earle and Miriam Erez (San Francisco: New Lexington Press, 1986), 539-540.

"Thank you," he said. "Within the confines of a given culture there is an underlying set of values that is comprised of the shared motives, values, beliefs, identities, and interpretations or meanings of significant events that result from common experiences of members or collectives that are transmitted across generations.[27] Culture has a degree of permanency in that its core remains relatively intact throughout generations. As such, it remains identifiable and distinguished from other cultures even amid changes that naturally occur over time. Culture has been described as like an onion." He advanced the slide and displayed another diagram. "At a culture's core are values that are expressed as practices. The outermost layer is comprised of symbols—words and gestures typically understood by members of the culture."[28]

He paused and glanced around the room. "What are some of the practices at the Company that only people who work here would understand?"

"Parking," a young man said.

"What does that mean?" he asked.

He elaborated, "Only a few people have designated parking spaces. However, don't even think about parking along the building in the side lot. Oh, no, sir. That's for managers." Everyone was nodding. *Really?* I thought. *Of course I had a parking space in front of the building, so how would I know?*

"Interesting," the Consultant said. "Values can be thought of as the invisible part of culture manifested through cultural practices, consisting of symbols, heroes, and rituals. Consider the relationship between culture, values, and practices as illustrated in the *Onion Diagram*,"— he advanced to the next slide—"such that cultural values drive practices.[29] Therefore, values are the driving force of a culture. They shape it, define it, and distinguish it from other cultures. This applies to organizations as well. While values have an individual component, they also exist collectively within a culture. Cultures tend to be either individualist or collectivist."

He paused for a moment. "Who can give me an example of an individualist culture?"

"The United States," a man said.

"Excellent," he said. "What makes us individualists?"

"Well," he said, "individuals strive for a high quality of life that is a result of success (on the individual level). Achievement, self-actualization, and self-respect characterize an individualistic society and also characterize self-esteem and self-actualization in Maslow's hierarchy of needs."[30]

"Great point," he exclaimed. "And thank you for referring back to Maslow's hierarchy of needs. I can see the small group session was effective." He smiled. "What is an example of a collectivist culture?" he asked.

"China," a lady at my table said.

"Yes. You're right on the money. Collectivist societies revolve around a tight social framework where differences exist between in-groups and out-groups. People expect to be looked after by their in-groups, which can consist of relatives, clans, or organizations in exchange for absolute loyalty.[31] While value formation tends to be more of an individual process, the type of culture in which one lives will have significant influence on their overall development. What kind of culture does the Company have, individualist or collectivist?" he asked.

There was an almost simultaneous, unanimous "individualist" response. Everyone, it seemed, was in agreement about that. *I guess, we're all out for ourselves,* I thought. The Consultant just smiled. I'm sure he expected that response.

"So culture implies some level of shared meaning, of a commonality in the way in which behavior is evaluated, right?" asked a member from table trust.

"Yes," he said. "However, an individual's behavior at any given moment may or may not be congruent with shared cultural meanings.[32] An individual's culture is an amalgam of beliefs, practices, and values that serves as a guide—loosely, in some cases—of what is acceptable within the confines of its construct. Individualist cultures focus on *me*, whereas collectivist cultures focus on *we*. However, this doesn't mean there aren't individualist living in collectivist cultures and vice versa. It simply describes the overall culture and general expectations of those in it."

"How do you quantify the difference?" a young lady asked.

"Well," he began. "Individualism stands for a society in which the ties between individuals are loose: Everyone is expected to look after her/his immediate family only. Collectivism stands for a society in which people from birth onwards are integrated into strong, cohesive in-groups, which throughout people's lifetime continue to protect them in exchange for unquestioning loyalty."[33]

"But the core of either type of culture is comprised of values, right?" asked a man from table honesty.

"Yes. Regardless of the society type, values lie at the core of its composite. The cultural composition one is exposed to will have a significant impact on one's value development.

Conversely, as individual values change, they will be reflected within the culture in a simultaneous duality, where each changes independently of one another, yet provides a direct impact on the other." He returned to the podium.

"Okay," he said checking the clock on the wall. "It's time for our afternoon break and small group meeting. Group leaders, please see me before you proceed." I wasn't the leader of the small group this afternoon, which was nice. That task fell to the facilities manager.

If the Situation Fits

After grabbing coffee, my group members and I sat in the training room and chatted about the afternoon's discussion while we waited for the facilities manager. I asked the people in my group about the parking situation. They eagerly informed me that it was in fact true that members of upper management "guarded" their spots and were quick to reprimand anyone who parked in their spaces. *I'll have to do something about that*, I thought.

The facilities manager entered, sat, opened the folder, and said, "Okay. I hope I do as good of a job at this as you did, Cheryl."

I smiled reassuringly. "You'll be fine."

"All right. We're going to discuss situational values." He opened the folder and read from the instructions.

"Do values exist individually or collectively?" he asked.

"Both," the account executive said.

"I agree," I said.

"Me too," the shipping clerk affirmed.

The receptionist nodded.

He read, "We must keep in mind that values do not singularly exist within an individual. Values exist individually, collectively, and institutionally. Therefore, it is conceivable that particular situations will elicit a different value response. This is based in part on the theory that values can be classified and divided interpretively." He looked up. "That sounds pretty complicated," he mused.

"Well," the account executive said, "I think what the article's saying is that we act according to our values and to the situation."

"Yes," I said. "That sums it up pretty good."

He pulled five copies of a diagram from the folder and gave us each one. We all looked at the chart and read its explanation.

> Schwartz identified fifty-six value items that can be grouped into ten value types, which can be further clustered into four value orientations: 1) *self-transcendence* (the altruistic value types of universalism and benevolence), 2) *self-enhancement* (egoistic values focused on personal power and achievement), 3) *openness* (including the value types of self-direction, hedonism and stimulation), and 4) *conservation* (including the tradition, conformity and security value types) (figure 3).[34]

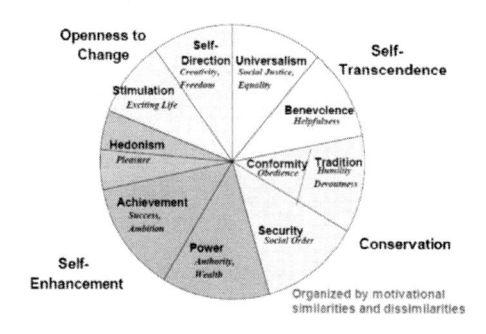

[Figure 3: A circular diagram labeled "Organized by motivational similarities and dissimilarities" showing value types arranged around a circle. The segments include: Self-Direction (Creativity, Freedom), Universalism (Social Justice, Equality), Benevolence (Helpfulness), Conformity (Obedience), Tradition (Humility, Devoutness), Security (Social Order), Power (Authority, Wealth), Achievement (Success, Ambition), Hedonism (Pleasure), Stimulation (Exciting Life). Outer groupings: Openness to Change, Self-Transcendence, Conservation, Self-Enhancement.]

The facilities manager read from his instructions. "Complimentary value types are grouped together (i.e., universalism and benevolence). The pursuit of individual values can result in conflict (i.e., benevolence and hedonism), if one value orientation is incongruent with another in a given situation. Individuals typically possess many, if not all, of the values depicted in figure three. In a given situation, not all values apply equally, which results in situational values. The closer the values are on the circle, the more similar are their underlying motivations; the more distant are the values, the more antagonistic their underlying motivations.[35] Distant values can lead to conflict if they are directly pitted against one another. More often though, a situation dictates a dominant value orientation, which is what leads to situational values."

"In other words," broke in the Shipping Clerk, "we act according to who we are in a given situation, right?"

"Not necessarily," the Receptionist said. "I think it depends on what our dominant value type is in a given situation."

"I think you're right," I said. "I believe a dominant value type exists within all of us, in any situation. We gravitate to a certain value type pretty much on a regular basis, but in a particular situation, we might lean in a different direction."

The facilities manager looked relieved that a discussion had broken out.

"Does that mean a situation can change who we are?" asked the account executive. "And if it changes who we are because of how we act, isn't that really showing us who we are? I mean, how we act is who we are, right?"

"I don't think that's true all the time," the receptionist said. "People make mistakes. They act on impulse or get caught up in something they shouldn't, but that doesn't necessarily define who they are, nor does it exemplify their dominant value type."

"I agree," the shipping clerk said. "Values can fluctuate based on the situation and based on how someone is feeling. Someone could be in a bad mood or angry and act out of character for their dominant value type. People act out of character on occasion."

"Okay," the facilities manager said, getting us back on track. "I think we're on the same page. Although a situation may lend itself to a particular value orientation, this does not eliminate the possibility for value conflict." He read from the file, "People act according to their values, because there is a need for consistency between one's beliefs and one's actions.[36] Within the values domains on your handout, there is a particular harmony and compatibility." We all studied the handout.

He removed a sheet of paper from the folder and read it.

"Both power and achievement emphasize social superiority and esteem. Achievement and hedonism are both concerned with self-indulgence. Affectively pleasant arousal is pursued both by hedonism and stimulation. Stimulations and self-direction both involve intrinsic motivation for mastery and openness to change. Reliance on one's own judgment and comfortableness with the diversity of existence are expressed both through self-direction and universalism. Universalism and benevolence are both concerned with enhancement of others and transcendence of selfish interests. Tradition and conformity both stress self-restraint and submission. Conformity and security both protect order and harmony. Security and power both stress avoiding or overcoming the threat of uncertainties by controlling relationships and resources."[37]

"In other words, values exist as a delicate balance within the four value orientations identified on the handout, correct?" the Account Manager asked.

"Yes," the facilities manager said. "I think you are correct. Conflict is generated in situations that oppose one another and decisions are made based on which values best fit the situation. In any given situation, people will act in accordance with the values that are the truest representation of themselves."

"Essentially," I said, "people gravitate to one value orientation over another because it most readily corresponds with their personality and worldview, and it assuages their conscience."

"Right," the facilities manager said. He continued as he skimmed the sheet. "Values directly contribute to the development of a worldview. I'm quoting, 'Our worldview forms the context within which we organize and build our understanding of reality,'[38] end quote." He looked up and paused. A worldview is the lens through which we see life. Quoting again, 'Our worldview forms the context within, which we organize and build our understanding of reality,'[39] end quote. We view and interpret the world in light of our worldview, we label situations and actions as right or wrong based on our worldview, we make decisions with regard to our view of the world. Our worldview is central to who we are and is a reflection of our values that manifests itself through the actions of our conscience."

"What you're saying is that values form our worldview, and our worldview determines how we see the world. So in reality, our values determine how we act and how we see the world," said the receptionist.

"Yes," he said. "It would appear that we act based on how we think we should act, and that is based on our worldview."

"And our worldview is comprised of our values, right?" she asked.

"Yes," he said.

"Hmm," she said. "Then what we're really saying is our values determine how we should act because we need consistency between the two, which makes sense. I mean, why act one way if it's not in alignment with your values, right?"

"I'll take this one," I said. "People often act in violation of their values because they believe that's what they're supposed to do, base on the situation. For example, have you ever thrown a soda can in the regular trash and not in the recycled bin?"

"Yeah, I guess I've made that mistake before when I was in a hurry. Who hasn't?"

"Did you take the time to take it out of the trash and put it in the correct bin?" I asked.

She hesitated a moment. "No."

"Okay, then," I continued, "that's an example of a situation in which you didn't act in accordance with your values. Why didn't you put the can in the correct bin?"

"I didn't want to take the time," she said

I smiled reassuringly. "It's not a big deal. I'm just making my point."

"I get what you're saying," she said, "and I see your point. Actions don't always align with values depending on the situation."

We wrapped up our small group discussions and headed back to the main training room for our final group discussion of day one.

The Human Conscience

"Okay," the Consultant said. "How was your small group discussion?"

"Great," one person said.

"Super," another said.

"Very good," the Consultant said. Again, he spent several minutes reviewing the subject of our small group discussion. For the most part, we all agreed values could vary depending on the situation. There were a few dissenters in the group who disagreed. He said, "On your tables, you will find a case study. Read it and then we'll discuss it as a group. I read the case study.

Case Study: The Aryan Brotherhood

One could hardly imagine members of a violent prison gang having values similar to his own. "The Aryan Brotherhood [is] a violent white supremacist gang that was formed in California prisons in the late 1960s."[40] For decades, it operated solely within the confines of prison walls throughout the country. Michael Thompson entered the California Penal System in 1975 and quickly became one of the Brotherhood's leading enforcers, killing over twenty fellow inmates. Thompson stated, "Killing is not something to take lightly. It's not something I'm proud of, but it's a reality. It's a reality based on this environment, and it's brutal."[41]

Casper Crowell was another of the Brotherhood's enforcers. He, too, has killed fellow inmates on behalf of the organization. Both Thompson and Crowell turned their backs on the organization and agreed to testify against the Brotherhood. Crowell's betrayal of the organization was due his belief they are nothing but "race traders," who take advantage of the racial disparity that exists in prison in order to exercise control over their cartel. He walked away from the organization because he had sworn to protect his fellow white inmates and was instead killing them. In regard to his incarceration, he remarked, "Everybody in here— the good, the bad, the ugly—we were all once somebody's little bundle of joy."[42] He emotionally recounted the grisly details of his violent deeds and even had tears well up in his eyes as he said, "I can imagine what little kids must be thinking—that I stole their daddy from them. I deserve to be here."[43] Crowell concluded by stating he woke up one day and realized, "What I'm involved with is bad."[44]

Thompson turned against the Brotherhood for a different reason. Steve Barnes, a long-time member of the organization who was currently incarcerated, was going to testify against them. He was placed in protective custody within the prison for his safety. Knowing they couldn't get to him, the leadership council of the Brotherhood decided to go after his family. Curtis Price was a Brotherhood member who was about to be paroled. He was tasked with assassinating Barnes' family. During the leadership council meeting, Thompson was the only member who voted against the plot. In response to this incident and the resulting murders, he turned against the group and testified against them, claiming he believed he had a responsibility to combat that which he created. He stated,

>*When you take somebody out there—a child, parents, a woman—when you say, 'I'm going to kill her to make an example'—whoa, wait a minute, wait a minute. Uh-uh, not me, not me. I don't do that. That goes beyond what I'm willing to do as a human being. I don't have a problem with violence at all with those who understand what it's about, but I will not and cannot tolerate violence against children, women, or elders in any capacity, in any shape, in any form.*[45]

Perhaps the capacity for value development and evolution exists within us all regardless of how heinous our deeds might be. Thompson ended his interview with these words:

>*I always thought I was a pretty good guy, but when you stop and really look at yourself, you find out you're not all that cool. You've got some real faults here that you need to look at. Maybe I'm in prison for a good reason.*[46]

After everyone finished reading the case study, the Consultant said, "Some of you might be wondering how this case study is germane to our conversation." A few people nodded. I didn't nod, but I had been wondering that myself. "Well," he continued, "what I find incredibly remarkable about this, which is a true story by the way, is how such hardened criminals could have a change of heart. I believe this case study illustrates the existence of the human conscience and deep-seated values." He paused as he began to walk around the room. "Thompson's words reflect self-awareness and the recognition of the human conscience. They ring true for everyone, because we all have faults. At the same time, they also provide evidence for the existence of values regardless of the confines in which they exist whether in society at-large or inside prison walls. Did this case study surprise anyone?" Many heads were nodding. "So what does this case study imply?" he asked.

A man at table trust said, "Thompson's actions support the contention that knowledge of right and wrong, or a semblance thereof, resides in all of us. Crowell and Thompson experienced conflicting values in which a particular situation determined a preferred course of action that deviated from their normal behavior, which seems strange to me given the circumstances. But I think, this course of action is evidence of the human conscience's existence."

"Absolutely," he said. "But is it true that we all have a conscience? I've heard people described as having no conscience. Is that true?"

A young woman said, "Many might argue that everyone has a conscience, an inner voice that guides behavior and decision-making based on absolute values innate to us all. The conscience is that part of our being that helps us distinguish right from wrong. It's an internal compass."

"Yes," he said. "What else?"

An older gentleman said, "Some, of course, would cite egregious acts against humanity as evidence against the existence of the human conscience, which is the 'development, maintenance, and application of generalizable [sic], internal standards of conduct or one's behavior.'[47] This implies a conscience is an innate human trait that is developed over time. It also indirectly infers that the fiber necessary for its development is internally present. That is, we are born with a conscience, or at the very least, born with the ability to develop a conscience."

"You are right on point," the Consultant said. "Such an assertion is a simplification of the complexity that is the human conscience, which is both complex and multifaceted and likely includes a number of unique (although, likely interrelated) skills, including moral emotions (such as guild, shame, empathy), internal regulators of behavior, and moral reasoning."[48] He let his words sink in. "The conscience has been perceived as integral to one's emotional and intellectual core and the mechanism by which we engage with *natural law*. That is, the law of God imprinted on the human heart.[49] Conscience thus formulates moral obligation in the light of the natural law: it is the obligation to do what the individual, through the workings of his conscience, knows to be a good he is called to do here and now.[50] In this sense, the human conscience is the reflection of God in all of us, an innate ability to recognize right and wrong and so distinguish one from the other."

"Not everyone believes in that reflection," a young man said. "Many deny the existence of God or a supreme being, which negates this stipulation."

"You're right," the Consultant said as he looked down and read from a document. "Freud did not believe in the existence of an original, natural capacity to distinguish good from bad. For him, there is no universal moral law derived from an inner morality, the sort reflected in the Old Testament statement 'I will put my law in their minds and write it on their heart.'[51] Freud believed man's capacity to distinguish right from wrong was a result of one's environment and sociological factors. However, popular views stipulate conscience is the inherent ability of every healthy human being to perceive what is right and wrong and, on the strength of this perception, to control, monitor, evaluate and execute their actions.[52] This stipulation quantifies the conscience based on two modifiers, perception and health—presumably, mental health. It postulates the idea not only that right and wrong exist, but also that each one can be perceived and distinguished from the other."

One woman barked, "A conscience is the autonomous development of a reasonably coherent set of internalized, other-regarding moral values and action-guiding principles based on them, and a commitment to act on them as overriding.[53] The phrase *Let your conscience be your guide* comes to mind. Am I close?"

"Correct," he said. "However, 'consciences vary radically from person to person and time to time; moreover, they are often altered by circumstance, religious belief, childhood, and training.'[54] Conscience serves as an internal behavior guide that is based on our values. Within the confines of society, conscience is a collective set of beliefs that governs general behavior."

"I agree," she said. She continued, "Conscience is an inner voice of special moral illumination or expertise and of incontrovertible moral authority, which reveals itself inwardly and unavoidably in conscience and warns us to do good and avoid evil and condemns us when we fail."[55]

"Absolutely," the Consultant said. "The conscience is akin to the angel on one shoulder and the devil on the other, when faced with moral decision. Good versus evil incarnate, if you will. The deciding factor rests in one's values, which to a large extent are believed to be good. Values fuel the conscience. So by the use of his conscience (heart) man knows how to act, and by the use of his reason he knows what to do.[56] In this regard, the conscience is the awareness of values in the presence of moral confrontation, and it is the conscience that provides, or should provide, clear direction to make the *right* choice when faced with the proverbial fork in the road."

We wrapped up our discussion, and the Consultant informed us we were to answer a series of questions that directly related to leadership. "At the conclusion of each day of training," he began, "you are going to form back into your small groups and answer five questions that are based on critical thinking, which is judicious reasoning about what to believe and, therefore, what to do.[57] Critical thinking is important, because people who engage in critical thinking tend to be able to provide evidence and reasoning for the opinions they hold."[58]

He displayed a slide that contained the five questions we were to answer. We were instructed that one person could record the answers, but we were to discuss them as a group. Everyone was to participate. Once we had finished answering them, we were free to go. He then gathered his things and left, telling us he would see us tomorrow.

> LEADERSHIP APPLICATION
>
> - What is the issue?
>
> - What are the implications for The Company?
>
> - Why does it matter?
>
> - How can The Company increase awareness of its core values?
>
> - If core value awareness increases, what would be the result?

Leadership Application

All the small groups divided among the tables. My small group gathered at my table. The receptionist agreed to write down our answers. At first, everyone started talking and we didn't get anywhere. Then we went around the table and took turns answering the questions. We concluded that values matter simply because we all have them. We bring them to work with us. They influence how we interact with others, how we perceive situations, and what actions we will take.

In an organizational setting, individual values may not always align with organizational values. Companies have developed core values and mission statements to bridge the gap between personal values and organizational values, guide employees in their daily actions, and identify expected behavior; the opposite of which might lead to disciplinary action and/or termination. At the end of the day, the receptionist listed our responses in order.

1. Everyone has values that may not align with The Company's values.
2. Misalignment could lead to unwanted behavior.
3. Unwanted behavior could breed a culture of acceptance.
4. The Company could display its core values more prominently and promote them throughout the year.

5. An increase in core value awareness might curb unwanted behavior and align the culture with core values.

After everyone left, I headed back to my office to check e-mails and phone messages. The Consultant was waiting for me in my office. "So how do you think it went today?" he asked.

"Well," I began, "I definitely learned a few things. I had no idea employees felt that way about the Company or that we had those kinds of problems."

"Yes, one of the disadvantages of being at the top of the organization is that often, one is unaware of what is happening at the lower levels."

"You got that right," I said. "How do I fix it?"

"Let's not worry about that right now. You need all the pieces of the puzzle so you can see the whole picture. Then you can tackle the main problem."

"Which is?" I prodded.

"We don't know yet," he said as he switched on his iPad. He tapped the screen a few times.

"What are you doing?" I asked.

"Looking at the Company's Facebook page. I want to see if anyone posted anything about today's training."

Hmm, I thought. *There's something I hadn't thought about before.*

"Why don't you post something about it?" he suggested.

"Me? Well, I don't usually make posts on the Company's Facebook page."

"Yes, I noticed." He smiled.

I took his point. "Okay," I said. "I see your point. I will."

"Great," he said, placing the iPad in his briefcase and rising. "I will see you tomorrow. Have a good night."

I sat and thought about what to write. The PR department usually updated the page. This was something new for me, but I wrote a few lines about the training and how much I enjoyed it, then stated that I had learned a few things.

I read a few e-mails and checked my voice mail. Before logging off, curiosity got the best of me, and I logged back in to Facebook. Three people had *liked* my post, and one person from the training group commented, "I thought it was good too. Good to have the 'boss' there."

"It's good to be there!" I replied with a smiley emoticon.

DAY 2
ETHICAL BOUNDARIES

Ethics is knowing the difference between what you have a right to do and what is right to do.

—Potter Stewart

Defining Ethics and Their Purpose

"Good morning," the Consultant said as everyone got settled. "Yesterday, we discussed the origin and definition of values and how they develop from early childhood through adolescence and into adulthood. What were some of answers you came up with in regard to the leadership application yesterday?"

We spent several minutes reviewing our end-of-day wrap-up answers. The Consultant reviewed the daily climate assessment responses. All tables had agreed that the training was beneficial, easy to follow, and applicable to their work environment.

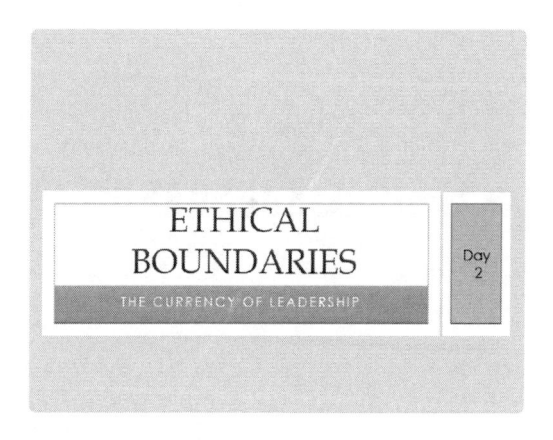

ETHICAL BOUNDARIES
THE CURRENCY OF LEADERSHIP
Day 2

The Consultant continued, "Values are the fundamental building blocks of ethics, which is today's topic. Ethics are a normative set of behavior standards within society. Ethics exist within a system and are 'a set of interrelated values concerning preferable modes of conduct.'[59] They are the behavioral manifestation of values that occur in the decision-making phase of life. Ethics comes from the Greek word *ethos*, which means the custom or way of life.[60]

He paused as he moved about the room. "What are some of the ways we use the term *ethical?*" he asked.

"Ethical behavior," one person said.

"Ethical standards."

"Ethical conduct."

"Great answers! Ethical behavior is linked to one's moral values."[61] He was at the podium now, looking down at his notes. "The *New Oxford American Dictionary* defines ethics as a set of moral principles, especially ones relating to or affirming a specified group, field, or form of conduct." He flashed a slide onto the screen and said, "Here are some of your definitions, extracted from the survey you took." We all read them to ourselves.

> ### SURVEY DEFINITIONS
>
> - Ethics are behavior that is consistent with values.
> - A desire to do the right thing.
> - Doing the right thing.
> - Behaving in a way that is honest and fair.
> - Behavioral display of values.
> - A moral principle or "value" held by an individual or in some cases a group that determines how they act -- it is the actual action that determines what their values are.

"Everyone rightly made the connection between values and ethics. Key points involved doing the right thing, behavior, and fairness. Ethics are action-oriented in that they require the outward manifestation of inward beliefs. They are a display of one's inner character. One can profess a particular belief (value.) However, the action one takes, or does not take, is indicative of genuine values."

"So values determine our behavior?" someone asked.

"Yes," he said. "And no. Can anyone think of a situation where one acts ethically but not in keeping with one's values?"

Everyone pondered this for a moment. Finally, a lady at the adjacent table said, "Well, if I were in the ladies' room with a coworker and found a wallet on the floor, I would be inclined to turn it in to the front desk, which is ethical. However, my normal action, according to my values, might have been to check it for money first, but I couldn't, since I wasn't alone. That's just an example, mind you. I'd never open a wallet I found," she insisted. We all laughed.

"Great example," the Consultant said. "You acted ethically, which is your behavior, yet it wasn't quite in keeping with your values." He paused and looked directly at her. "In your example—which was really good—, had you been alone, would you consider yourself a bad person for taking the money out of the wallet before turning it in to the front desk?"

She thought about the question for a minute. "Well, if I checked the ID and it belonged to someone I knew, I wouldn't take the money. But if it belonged to a stranger, I would, and I wouldn't consider myself a bad person."

"Why not?" he probed. "What's the difference if you know the person or not?"

"If the wallet belonged to a stranger, and I hate to sound like a child, but it's finders keepers. No one will know if I took the money. But if it were someone I knew, I'd feel bad."

"You'd still be acting unethically," a young man said somewhat heatedly. "It's still stealing. That's like saying it's okay to rob someone's house as long as you don't know who lives there."

"That's not the same thing at all," she protested. "I didn't steal the wallet. I found it."

"How do you define stealing?" he asked angrily.

She was fired up now. "Stealing involves intent, and I had no intent to steal the wallet. I didn't know it was there. I found it!"

A middle-aged lady at the same table chimed in, "Yes, but you made the conscious decision to take something that did not belong to you. That makes it stealing."

"Exactly," the young man added. "If you want to call it *finding* so you can sleep better at night, go ahead. It's still stealing!"

She stood up and pointed a finger at him, "I'm not calling it anything to make myself feel better! Anyone who finds money is going to take it, and if you say you wouldn't, you're lying."

Now he was on his feet. "Is that so? You think we're all dishonest and a bunch of thieves?"

"You wait just a minute, young man. I'm no thief!"

"Okay," the Consultant broke in. "I think this is a great discussion, and it's a great segue into our next topic. So let's keep that example in mind as we proceed throughout the day and see what we come up with in terms of examples from the Company."

He meandered around the room as he spoke. "As we consider ethics and the current discussion, let's keep in mind that ethics involves both terminal values (end-state values) and instrumental values (modes of conduct). Terminal values 'may be viewed as *ends* toward which one is striving. Instrumental values may be viewed as *means* that one will employ to achieve the ends.'"[62] He displayed a table on the screen.

TERMINAL VS. INSTRUMENTAL

Terminal Values	Instrumental Values
A prosperous life	Hard-working, aspiring
A stimulating, active life	Open-minded
Lasting contribution	Competent, effective
Free of war and conflict	Lighthearted, joyful
Beauty of nature and the arts	Neat, tidy

"Ideally, what this indicates is the end justifies the means in a manner that is conducive to both personally and socially accepted values. Essentially, ethics are moral rules that serve as the standard by which each person may judge his or her own actions.[63] And it is also a standard by which a person can judge the actions of others, which is very often the case as we have just seen. You will discuss this point further in your morning small groups."

He turned to the group and asked, "Are ethical standards universal?"

We thought about the question for a few minutes.

I spoke, "Ethical standards are a matter of individual and cultural application."

"So you don't think they are universal?" he asked.

"No, I don't."

"Well, you're not alone. The theory of ethical relativism posits the idea that whatever a culture thinks is right or wrong really is right or wrong for the members of that culture.[64] While this theory of ethical behavior might seem appealing on the surface, it lacks substance. Why do you suppose that is?"

A man from a back table said, "If ethics were a matter of relativity, there would hardly be a historical, definitive standard. I read an article that said, 'When early anthropologists probed beneath surface [of] moral disagreements, they often discovered agreement at deeper levels on more basic values.'[65] Essentially, people tend to agree about moral standards."

"Excellent!" he said. "You're referring to ethical absolutism, which is the theory that there is a single moral law that applies to everyone which is derived from common needs and reasoning."[66]

"If that theory were true, it would mean that ethics are, in fact, universal and would not vary from culture to culture, right?" asked the gentleman seated next to me.

"Correct. Detractors of this theory point to varying ethical practices as evidence against absolutism." The Consultant returned to the podium and read from his notes.

"The moral standard(s) may be common, but adherence may differ. Hence, we derive *perceived relativity*, but, in essence, all behavior is directed by common moral values that have been deemed, through experience, to be essential for successful continuation. In contrast to the dictums of ethical relativity and in respect to managers, Prasad and Rao have pointed out that certain ethical norms, such as honesty, integrity, self-discipline, loyalty and compassion, are perceived as basic moral standards and are widely proclaimed as part of many civilizations, yet adherence to those standards varies greatly."[67]

"So there are no absolutes?" the gentleman asked.

"While there are no clearly established ethical absolutes, there are universally accepted norms. To a certain extent, this negates the notion of relativism. Individual and cultural beliefs may vary. However, the existence of a common standard is generally present, regardless of the variation of beliefs."

He walked around the room slowly as she spoke. "Your survey data indicated that seventy percent of you believed ethics were not universal. Yet according to your responses, ethics are important for the following reasons." He projected another slide onto the screen, and we all read its contents silently. When we were finished, he asked, "So what purpose do ethics serve?"

> ### ETHICS' IMPORTANCE
>
> - They shine the light on the true character of a person or community.
> - Ethics promote fairness in society.
> - They establish accountability.
> - They help to create cohesion within a society.
> - Ethics make us credible before others and God.
> - A leader who exhibits behavior that is consistent with his or her values provides a model for other to follow and can reasonably require that they follow that model.

"Ethics right the ship, so to speak, and provide a cultural and universal standard of behavior," a woman said.

"They provide a framework of what is morally acceptable by the general populace as well as provide the standard by which to judge the actions of one's fellow man or woman," another person noted.

"Indeed," the Consultant said. "Ethics comprises complex ideas, applications, and interpretations about not only what is right and wrong, but also why things are considered right and wrong.[68] The application of ethics includes both conceptual and evaluative aspects in regard to action, particularly in a proactive sense." He had wandered back to the podium and read from his notes.

"Ethics should be proactive and prevent straying in the gray area, which can spread and morph into full-blown unethical behavior. That being said though, ethics needs to function more as a locked door to illicit behavior rather than simply as a Keep Out sign on an unlocked door. Curiosity has gotten the best of many who have wandered through the door and left their values and ethics behind, never to be seen again."[69]

One of the board members at the table across from mine said, "In other words, ethics are not only a standard by which we judge actions, as is so often the case; rather, they must serve as a guide that governs our lives and society and provides clear direction *before* we take action."

"Exactly!" he said. "Using them as a standard by which to judge action is indicative of the law, as we shall see later."

Today's morning session had gone faster than yesterday's. It was time for a break and our morning small group. I had to admit it, I enjoyed the small group discussions. I learned a lot about the company that I never knew previously.

Litany of Failures

It was the Receptionist's turn to lead the small group. Today's topic dealt with ethical failures. The receptionist read from the file, "The twentieth century has seen its share of ethical failures in all practically all industries—government, military, and corporate America. While the failures are many, the reasons are few. The ethical shortcomings were caused by the unraveling of the fabric that is human nature."

She passed out five copies of stapled documents. She continued, "Okay, according to the survey we took, we indicated the following reasons for ethical failures."

We reviewed the first page.

- o *A lack of moral character.*
- o *Lack of moral courage.*
- o *Greed and power.*
- o *Lack of integrity and honesty.*
- o *Behavior that is misaligned with values.*

"All right," the Receptionist began, "the handout lists several ethical failures that made the news. We are supposed to take turns reading them and then discuss them." We sat in silence and read.

- New York Gov. Eliot L. Spitzer's political future was thrown in doubt yesterday after he was identified as an anonymous client heard on a federal wiretap arranging to pay money and buy train tickets for a high-priced New York prostitute to meet him at a downtown Washington hotel. "I have acted in a way that violated the obligations to my family and that violate my, or any, sense of right and wrong," Spitzer,

48, said in a terse public statement, with his wife, Silda Wall Spitzer, at his side. "I have disappointed and failed to live up to the standard that I expect of myself."[70]

- Enron, once a sleepy natural gas pipeline company, grew to become the nation's seventh largest publicly held corporation. But its shoddy business practices, aided by bankers and advisors feeding from the gravy train, brought down the company in December 2001. Altogether, 16 former Enron execs including Skilling had been sentenced to prison. A lot of people have suffered, not the least of whom are the shareholders and pensioners who lost it all. Punishment serves as a deterrent. But a clear-cut mission and a corporate code of ethics are crucial. It's the foundation to which boards, managers and workers rely when they reach a fork in the road.[71]
- Capt. Shawn Hendricks, the head of the Navy program that manages the fleet's IT networks was fired June 24 after a "substantiated investigation … into an improper relationship and unprofessional behavior."[72]
- Cmdr. Edward White was removed as CO of Strike Fighter Squadron 106 on Aug. 26 due to "loss of confidence in his ability to command following the preliminary findings of an ongoing command investigation into an alleged inappropriate relation-

ship with a female Department of the Navy civilian employee."[73]

- William Jefferson Clinton was impeached on charges of perjury and obstruction of justice today by a divided House of Representatives, which recommended virtually along party lines that the Senate remove the nation's 42d President from office. At 1:22 p.m., the House of Representatives approved, 228 to 206, the first article of impeachment, accusing Mr. Clinton of perjury for misleading a Federal grand jury last Aug. 17 about the nature of his relationship with a White House intern, Monica S. Lewinsky. A second article of impeachment, charging Mr. Clinton with obstruction of justice, passed on a narrower vote of 221 to 212. It accused him of inducing others to lie in order to conceal his affair with Ms. Lewinsky.[74]

- Martin Sullivan realized that AIG was in severe trouble the firm and continued to make risky investments in order to drive short-term growth. AIG sold insurance on billions of dollars of debt securities backed by everything from corporate loans to subprime mortgages to auto loans to credit-card receivables. It promised buyers of the swaps that if the debt securities defaulted, the firm would pay these losses. The company further stated that if the prices of these securities collapsed, AIG would reacquire them. The majority of securities were called collateralized-debt obligations, or CDOs, that were backed by securities such as mortgage bonds. CDOs, in particular, were exceptionally complex, involving more than 100 securities, each backed by multiple mortgages, auto loans or credit-card receivables.[75]

When everyone had finished, the receptionist reviewed her instructions and said, "It seems that no matter where we look today, the erosion of ethics and basic moral principles of right and wrong have taken us to the point where trust in our institutions and the very systems that make our society work are in imminent danger of oblivion.[76] The evolution of society has not only increased the prevalence of ethical failures, it has also provided increased awareness of said failures via the proliferation of technology, which has provided instant access to information via social media applications."

She consulted the instructions again. "Okay, what are everyone's thoughts about the ethical failures?"

The facilities manager spoke first. "As a veteran, I can relate to the military failures. I've seen leaders rise to power and then abuse it, because they believe they are above the law."

"What I noticed," I said, "and I hate to sound this way, is that all of these examples involve senior male leaders. What are everyone's thoughts about that?"

The shipping clerk chimed in, "Well, I don't know what the statistics are, but I'd venture to say men occupy more leadership positions than women. Therefore, it seems logical if there are going to be failures, men would be the larger demographic."

The account executive said, "I get what you're saying, and mathematically, I suppose you're right. But I wonder what the numbers are for female leaders?"

"Yeah," the receptionist said. "We should ask the Consultant about that after lunch."

Everyone nodded in consent. We got back to the list of failures.

"What else did you observe about the failures?" the receptionist asked.

"Inappropriate relationships," the facilities manager stated.

"What do you mean by that?" the receptionist asked.

"I mean, the majority of these failures occurred by powerful leaders who had inappropriate relationships."

"In keeping with our discussion yesterday, I noticed the individuals didn't seem to possess good values. Their values (who they really were) revolved around themselves and their own interests," I said.

"You think they were bad to begin with?" asked the facilities manager.

"Well," I said, "to a certain extent, yes. I mean, when faced with making an ethical decision, everyone mentioned in the examples has a history or pattern of making unethical decisions. Anyone can make a mistake, but what does it mean when it happens again and again and again? What does that say about their values and who they really are?"

The account executive spoke. "You make a good point. I suppose, deep down, we all like to believe we know ourselves, but perhaps we never really know who we are until tested. Then our real values come out."

The receptionist nodded. "Yeah, I guess you're right."

The account executive said, "I've been in the corporate world for a long time. Ethical failures are fact, particularly in large organizations. Many organizations have adopted codes of ethics and core values in order to govern the behavior of their personnel as well as to clearly delineate expectations." *Interesting*, I mused. *We, too, have a code of ethics.*

"Such codes and values can be found in the most professional of environments," the facilities manager said. "The reason for the presence of these codes and values is because in a workplace without clearly defined core values, people naturally rely on their own values to guide them on how they interact with colleagues, direct reports, supervisors, customers, etc."[77]

"Agreed," I said. "Establishing ethical standards provides a baseline and reference of acceptable behavior in an effort to prevent unethical behavior, which can become contagious."

The receptionist read from the folder. "According to the survey, ninety percent of us agreed unethical behavior was contagious. It says here," she said, reading from the page.

"If unethical behaviors are known (or rumored) and the performer still gets rewards, it can create the impression that these bad behaviors are acceptable. In this way, one cheater can lead to more cheating by others. First, by creating a standard that can only be met by cheating, and second, by contributing to a belief that everyone is doing it."[78]

She looked up. "What does everyone think about that?"

"I agree," the shipping clerk said. "I'll be honest, if I see someone get away with something and not get punished, I might do it too. Like taking a roll of packing tape home. I've seen people do it many times. I've seen people mail personal packages from work on the Company's account. First, it's one person then it's another."

"I disagree," the account executive said firmly. "Unethical behavior might be contagious in some cases, but it still comes down to the individual to decide."

"Plus," the receptionist said, "some people may not see certain things as unethical behavior. In the example listed, people might take packing tape home and use the company's account, because they believe they have permission to, based on seeing others do it."

"That might be true," I said. "And I agree…to a point. I mean, where do you draw the line? It might be natural for someone to take a company pen home in his or her pocket and not think about it. After all, it's only a pen, and it's not going to break the Company. I can see how that kind of thinking could escalate into something like packing tape and shipping packages. But I believe, at some point, it has to register with the individual."

"It might not register if there isn't a clearly defined standard," the account executive said. "Which is probably why there have been so many ethical failures."

"Good point," the receptionist said. Reading from the folder she said, "Ethical failures plagued the latter half of the twentieth century. Perhaps unethical behavior did indeed become contagious. It has been observed that [individuals] working in organizations in which unethical behavior is widespread are more likely to make unethical decisions themselves."[79]

I had strong feeling about codes of ethics, and I spoke up. "Ethical codes and core values can be found in many organizations today, including ours. Their role is not only to thwart unethical behavior; rather, they serve as a catalyst to align thinking with a common standard."

"Good point," the receptionist said. She read a concluding statement from the folder. "The code of ethics must do more than hang on the company wall. Its new and improved role is to serve as a preventative measure. That is, ethics must regulate not only the behavior of individuals and organizations. It must also regulate their thinking in order to guide actions and prevent actions that have irrevocable consequences."[80]

"I agree," the account executive said. "Simply having a code isn't going to change anyone's behavior. It's got to be part of the organization's culture."

"And how would you make it part of the culture?" I asked, genuinely interested.

"Well, I would hold training and teach people what the Company expects in terms of conduct. Hold people accountable. If they can't behave, well, then they have to go. Bad behavior can't be swept under the carpet."

"Yeah," the shipping clerk said. "Maybe place the Company's code of ethics in the employee cafeteria and in the bathrooms."

"The bathrooms?" I asked surprised.

"Hey, it sounds crazy, but people go to the bathroom several times a day and stare at a blank wall or door. Why not put something there for them to read?"

Huh, I thought. *That's a brilliant idea.* And so I said. "I'll take that under advisement."

The shipping clerk smiled.

The receptionist looked at her watch and said, "Okay, everyone, it's time to go to lunch." Again, we all went to lunch together. Only this time, I took everyone to the executive lunchroom, where we continued to discuss ways to improve ethical behavior and create awareness of the Company's code of ethics.

Teaching Ethics

"Welcome back," the Consultant said. "Did everyone enjoy the morning's small group discussion?"

Everyone nodded and people said, "Yes," "Great discussion," "Very stimulating."

"Good," he said. "I am excited to hear it. Continuing with that theme, as a result of the many ethical failures in the latter half of the twentieth century, many business schools have begun including ethical training as part of their curriculum. Additionally, an increasing number of institutions are enhancing their commitment to the coverage of ethics in the business curriculum, in part, due to the unethical leadership uncovered at all levels of organizations."[81]

He walked around the room as he spoke. "This raises an interesting question. Can ethics and ethical behavior be taught? What do you think?"

"Sure," a man said. "You can teach it all day long. But will it change a person's behavior?"

"Ah," the Consultant said. "That's the million-dollar question. Can teaching ethics change an individual's behavior?"

"I think teaching ethics can ultimately change someone's behavior in the long run, as long as they understand the consequences."

"Consequences?" the Consultant asked. "What do you mean by consequences?"

"As we studied in our morning small groups, unethical behavior has consequences, and the consequences can act as a kind of deterrent that will produce ethical behavior."

"So the only reason to act ethically is because of the consequences of getting caught?" asked a man from table respect.

"No, that's not what I'm saying. I just think the fact there are consequences would reinforce ethical behavior. So teaching ethics might create more awareness and lead to more ethical behavior."

"Very intriguing," the Consultant said. "In regard to the recent ethical failures in corporate America, an article in *Forbes* addressed the idea of teaching ethics. There is a copy of it in your packet. Please take a moment to review it."

We all opened our packets and removed the copy of the article. It was very informative and went on to state:

> Because many of these international leaders have MBA's from the world's top business schools, a substantial debate has erupted regarding the role that business schools might have played in indirectly precipitating the crisis and how business schools can limit the possibility of future crises. Did business school curricula adequately prepare MBA students to face the ethical questions related to the business practices that brought us to the economic brink? Are the professors of the world's leaders responsible, in any way, for their individual or collective actions? It is encouraging to see, thus, that many schools, in response to the financial crisis, are updating their curricula to better prepare students for the ethical questions they may be forced to answer in the

decades to come. For example, the Aspen Institute and Yale School of Management created Giving Voice to Values, a business school curriculum that emphasizes "ethical implementation," focusing on how to stand up for one's values in the workplace. This curriculum is being piloted at over 50 institutions, including business schools at Stanford, Duke, INSEAD, and MIT, according to the Giving Voice to Values website. HBS and Columbia are also piloting the curriculum in addition to updating their own programs. Columbia reconfigured its curriculum this year to incorporate "analysis, decision making, and leadership." Additionally, HBS changed its decades-old curriculum in 2011. For first-year MBA students at Harvard, there is now a program called "Field Immersion Experiences for Leadership Development" where students have the opportunity to apply what they learned in class while working with industries abroad and building an entrepreneurial company in just six weeks. By including opportunities to practically apply ethical decision-making models, global MBA programs better prepare students for the challenges they will face in the business world.[82]

When we had all finished reading the article, the Consultant stated, "It seems that business schools believe they can tip the scales by training their students to make appropriate decisions when faced with an ethical challenge by allowing them to put theory into practice in a controlled environment. The last sentence of the quote above implies not only that ethical challenges lie beyond the walls of academia, but also that those very challenges often result in decisions that lead to ethical failures. This makes me wonder about the nature of such challenges and why they frequently lead to unethical outcomes versus ethical ones. What is it about the ethical fork in the road that makes individuals choose the unethical choice over the ethical one?"

A gentleman from table loyalty answered, "Perhaps the rationale for making unethical decisions lies in our nature. We desire to do the right thing, but for some inexplicable reason, we fail to make the right decision. Maybe we are the victims of society's sway, or perhaps our organizational environment exerts undue influence on us."

"Very true," the Consultant said as he returned to the podium. "That's where social influence comes in." He glanced down and read, "Aspects of organizational environments, including ethical codes, organizational culture, and coworker behavior, affect how employees respond to moral issues by exerting social influence. Social influence occurs when people change their thoughts, feelings, or behaviors in response to their environment keeping with their environment, and these can be broadly classified as obeying direct requests (compliance); copying others because their behavior is presumed to be the right response in a situation (informational conformity); and doing what others do in order to fit in (normative conformity)."[83]

He looked up and began to meander among the tables. "Whatever the case and whatever the reason, people make unethical choices. Why is that?"

"It may be due to a combination of factors, such as the social influence you mentioned. Or it could be due to the exertion of social power, which is an individual's capacity to modify others' states by providing or withholding resources or administering punishment,"[84] said a member from my table.

"Yes," the Consultant said. "Society, as well as organizations, is comprised of those who have power and those who do not. Power and its allure can be a key contributor to decision-making that could lead to unethical behavior."

He had wandered back to the podium where he read us another document. "Theory and research suggest that the experience of power has consequences for people's attention to external stimuli. The argument of the situated focus theory of power is that, because the powerful are less dependent on others for their outcomes, their attention is more focused on themselves. In contrast, the powerless focus their attention more on contextual stimuli, because they are objectively more dependent on external circumstances and need to increase the predictability of their environment. The greater attention to the self should lead the powerful to become more aware of their own personal thoughts and feelings."[85]

He began to slowly walk around the room again. "So what do think that means?"

"Essentially, power—the lack thereof or the desire for it—can lead to unethical behavior," I said.

"Yes," he said. "As such, organizations routinely conduct training on ethics and ethical behavior." He smiled. "Sounds familiar, right?" We all laughed.

"The question still remains though as to whether ethics can be taught. Research is dubious about the effectiveness of teaching ethics. Rather than preach about right and wrong to students, there is a preference to enlighten people in regard to their decision-making by posing a series of questions."

He displayed a slide on the screen. A member from each table took turns reading the questions.

QUESTIONS

- Have I looked at the problem from the perspective of all affected parties?
- Who will be helped, and who will be harmed?
- What alternative courses of action do I have?
- Which outcomes are consistent with my values and duties?
- What kind of results can I expect if the decision sets a precedent and becomes the general rule?
- Am I confident that my decision will seem as reasonable over a long period of time as it seems now?

Tony Buono, "Can Ethics Be Taught?"

When we had finished, the Consultant asked, "What do you think? Do you believe asking this series of questions can curb unethical behavior and that using them can actually teach ethics?"

"I don't know if ethics can be taught. Another interesting criticism of ethics is that, as long as we have laws that dictate what is permissible, we do not need courses in ethics."[86]

"That is an interesting perspective in that it places the burden of ethical behavior on the law and bases its existence on the consequences of non-conformity, as we have discussed."

"In other words," a middle-aged lady said, "unethical behavior has consequences, thereby making it a form of crime and punishment. Thus the presence of ethics should be obvious as indicated by those who have experienced the negative consequences of behaving unethically."

"Yes," the Consultant said. "While this may seem somewhat logical, the fallacy lies in the assumption that the law exists to enforce ethical standards. It exists to establish and enforce legal standards, which may coincide to a great extent with ethical standards. However, as you might recall, many a trial ended in legal fairness while, at the same time, leaving room for ethical debate."

He paused as he returned to the podium. He continued, "Over ninety percent of you indicated you had received ethical training during the course of your careers. Ethical training is gaining momentum in organizations including the government. For example, this week [July 2014], United States Representatives Scott Rigell (VA-02) and David Cicilline (RI-01) introduced the Ensuring Trust and Honorability In Congressional Standards (ETHICS) Act, bipartisan legislation that would require all members of the House of Representatives to undergo mandatory ethics training. Currently, all senators, senate staff, and house staff are required to take ethics training every year. Specifically, the ETHICS Act would make ethics training and awareness programs mandatory for house members, delegates and the resident commissioner of the House of Representatives beginning January 3, 2015.

"In addition,

- Training must be completed no later than 60 days after starting service, and;
- Training must be completed during each new session of Congress beginning with the 1st session of the 114th Congress."[87]

We concluded the morning session by acknowledging the teaching of ethics resulted from a litany of ethical failures that occurred on a scale of unprecedented magnitude. Universities, corporations, and the government have adopted ethical codes and implemented training programs to promote awareness and better decision-making. Yet, for all of their efforts, unethical behavior still occurs. Utilizing training programs like this one and curriculum may have brought ethics to the forefront of learning and education, but it in and of itself is not a cure-all or solution.

It was time to head into our second small group of the day to continue our discussion.

Dilemmas

The account executive was slated to lead the afternoon small group. He entered the room and reviewed the group folder.

"Okay," he said, glancing at the folder. "Ethical dilemmas are typically representative of self-interest and self-preservation at the expense of another individual or group of individuals. We're going to take a look at some scenarios, which the Consultant told the group leaders are often skewed in light of this perspective. They are intended to illustrate the concept of a greater good or a more ethical choice regardless of the consequences." He gave each of us a sheet of paper with scenarios on the front and back. He continued, "As such, scenarios are frequently the subject of debate when studied."

"This should be a fun meeting," the shipping clerk interjected. We all laughed for moment, then the account executive continued, "According to the survey data, almost all of us indicated we have been faced with an ethical dilemma, and seventy-five percent of us believe there is a correct answer/solution to an ethical dilemma."

He looked up at the group and said, "We are supposed to review the ethical dilemmas I passed out and use the "Three Step Method" on this sheet." He passed out another sheet that contained the following information:

Step One: Analyze the Consequences

Okay, so you're going to stay on this side of the law. What next? It's probably easier to start by looking at the consequences of the actions you're considering.

Assume you have a variety of options. Consider the range of both positive and negative consequences connected with each one.

1. Who will be helped by what you do?
2. Who will be hurt?
3. What kind of benefits and harms are we talking about? After all, some "goods" in life (like health) are more valuable than others (like a new VCR). A small amount of "high quality" good can outweigh a larger amount of "lower quality" good. By the same token, a small amount of "high quality" harm (the pain you produce if you betray someone's trust on a very important matter) can outweigh a larger amount of "lower quality" pain (the disappointment connected with waiting another few months for a promotion).

4. How does all of this look over the long run as well as the short run? And if you're tempted to give short shrift to the long run, just remember that you're living with a lot of long-term negative consequences (like air and water pollution and the cost of the S&L bailout) that people before you thought weren't important enough to worry about.

After looking at all of your options, which one produces the best mix of benefits over harms?

Step Two: Analyze the Actions

Now consider all of your options from a completely different perspective. Don't think about the consequences. Concentrate instead strictly on the actions. How do they measure up against moral principles like honesty, fairness, equality, respecting the dignity of others, respecting people's rights, and recognizing the vulnerability of individuals weaker or less fortunate than others? Do any of the actions that you're considering "cross the line," in terms of anything from simple decency to an important ethical principle? If there's a conflict between principles or between the rights of different people involved, is there a way to see one principle as more important than the others?

What you're looking for is the option whose actions are least problematic.

Step Three: Make a Decision

And now, take both parts of your analysis into account and make a decision.

This strategy should give you at least some basic steps you can follow.[88]

The Ethical Dilemmas
The Hostage Ecologists

Tom is part of a group of ecologists who live in a remote stretch of jungle. The entire group, which includes eight children, has been taken hostage by a group of paramilitary terrorists. One of the terrorists takes a liking to Tom. He informs Tom that his leader intends to kill him and the rest of the hostages the following morning.

He is willing to help Tom and the children escape, but as an act of good faith he wants Tom to torture and kill one of his fellow hostages whom he does not like. If Tom refuses his offer, all the hostages including the children and Tom will die. If he accepts his offer, then the others will die in the morning but Tom and the eight children will escape.

Should Tom torture and kill one of his fellow hostages in order to escape from the terrorists and save the lives of the eight children?

The Life Insurance Policy

Mary is in a hospital lounge waiting to visit a sick friend. A young man sitting next to Mary explains that his father is very ill. The doctors believe that he has a week to live at most. He explains further that his father has a substantial life insurance policy that expires at midnight.

If his father dies before midnight, this young man will receive a very large sum of money. He says that the money would mean a great deal to him and his family, and that no good would come from his father's living a few more days. After talking with him Mary can tell this man is in desperate need of the money to feed his family. The man asks Mary to go up to his father's room and smother his father with a pillow.

Should Mary kill this man's father in order to get money for the man and his family?

The Submarine Crew

Mark is a crewperson on a marine-research submarine traveling underneath a large iceberg. An onboard explosion has damaged the ship, killed and injured several crewmembers. Additionally, it has collapsed the only access corridor between the upper and lower parts of the ship. The upper section, where Mark and most of the others are located, does not have enough oxygen remaining for all of them to survive until Mark has reached the surface. Only one remaining crewmember is located in the lower section, where there is enough oxygen.

There is an emergency access hatch between the upper and lower sections of the ship. If released by an emergency switch, it will fall to the deck and allow oxygen to reach the area where Mark and the others are. However, the hatch will crush the crewmember below, since he was knocked unconscious and is lying beneath it. Mark and the rest of the crew are almost out of air though, and they will all die if Mark does not do this.

Should Mark release the hatch and crush the crewmember below to save himself and the other crewmembers?

The Overloaded Lifeboat

Doug is on a cruise ship when there is a fire on board, and the ship has to be abandoned. The lifeboats are carrying many more people than they were designed to carry. The lifeboat he's in is sitting dangerously low in the water—a few inches lower and it will sink.

The seas start to get rough, and the boat begins to fill with water. A group of old people are in the water and ask Doug to throw them a rope so they can come aboard the lifeboat. It seems to Doug that the boat will sink if it takes on any more passengers.

Should Doug refuse to throw the rope in order to save himself and the other lifeboat passengers?

The Unfaithful Wife

You are an emergency worker that has just been called to the scene of an accident. When you arrive you see that the car belongs to your wife. Fearing the worst you rush over, only to see she is trapped in her car with another man. He is obviously her lover, with whom she's been having an affair.

You reel back in shock, devastated by what you have just found out. As you step back, the wreck in front of you comes into focus. You see your wife is seriously hurt and she needs attention straight away. Even if she gets immediate attention there's a very high chance she'll die. You look at the seat next to her and see her lover. He's bleeding heavily from a wound to the neck and you need to stem the flow of blood immediately.

If you attend to your wife, her lover will bleed to death, and you may not be able to save her anyway. If you work on the lover, you can save his life, but your wife will definitely die.

Who should you choose to work on?

"So," the account executive said, "what does everyone think?"

"I think these are interesting, but c'mon, who could really do some of these things?" asked the shipping clerk.

"I agree," the receptionist added. "And even if we sit here and say what we could do, how would we really know that unless we were in that situation?"

"True," I said. "I was just thinking the same thing. This is a great exercise, but in the end, we'll never know what we'll do until we have to make a choice."

"Exactly," the facilities manager said. "These steps might lead us to make a decision that seems *right* but in the end, there really isn't a right choice. There's only a choice that's less wrong."

"How is self-preservation wrong, especially if someone is going to die anyway?" asked the account executive.

"You make it sound cut and dry," the facilities manager said. "I suppose when faced with saving our own lives, we might surprise ourselves with our actions, but I don't think it's as cut and dry as you make it sound."

"I don't mean to make it sound that way, but we have the instinct to survive. Fight or flight, right?"

"I suppose so," the shipping clerk said. "But I wouldn't want to have to make a decision like that."

I said, "Ethical dilemmas present a challenge to make a decision that potentially benefits one person or a group of people, while at the same time, harming another, physically, mentally, or emotionally. Most people, I suppose, will employ a rationale system to arrive at what seems to be a logical and right conclusion."

Everyone nodded in agreement. *This was an interesting conversation,* I thought.

We concluded that while such a process might be reasonable and beneficial, a decision must be made and the consequences suffered. This process draws into question the concept of a *right* decision versus a *wrong* decision and concludes that through careful analysis, an individual can make a *right* decision when faced with an ethical dilemma. The implication is that a *right* decision to an ethical dilemma, in fact, exists. Seventy-five percent of survey respondents believe there is a *right* answer or solution to an ethical dilemma. This may be true when presented with a scenario, such as the ones above; however, in real life, making a decision that has permanent, detrimental consequences and living with it is not quite so cut and dry. Certainly, making a decision that benefits many while only harming one or a few seems logical and rational. Such thinking implies a greater good exists, and that the greater-good benefit justifies that decision. In other words, ethical decisions that benefit the majority are *right*, because the greater good has more value than that of the minority.

A Greater Good

"Well," the Consultant began, "how was your small group discussion? Did you find the ethical dilemmas challenging?"

Almost at once, everyone started talking about the ethical dilemmas. It was clear the group was divided as to whether there was a *right* answer to an ethical dilemma. The Consultant just stood silently and listened to the conversation. After a while, it fizzled out, and he continued.

"The ethical dilemmas were designed to make you think about whether or not a greater good exists." As was his custom, he began to walk around the room. "Is there such a thing as *the greater good* as the ethical dilemmas imply?" This question sparked more conversation at individual tables. In fact, some conversations spilled over to other tables. We all debated the question in a chaotic cacophony for several minutes.

Finally, the Consultant interrupted, "Can one make a decision with both a negative and positive outcome in which the positive outcome outweighs the negative?" This time our responses were more orderly.

"On paper, sure, but real life is another thing," said a woman from table compassion.

"Real life is another thing," a gentleman from table trust said. "But there is a greater good sometimes. It's harsh, but it's true. We just don't like to admit it, because somehow we believe it's still an unethical decision."

"I see," the Consultant said. "So right is right and wrong is wrong, regardless of the circumstances, correct?"

The gentleman maintained his position. "Yes."

"So it's better to make the right decision and let everyone suffer, rather than make the wrong decision and protect others?" he asked.

"I'm not saying that," the gentleman protested.

"I don't agree with that," I said. "Sometimes, you can do something that is, well…less right than you'd like it to be, but it's nevertheless right in the grand scheme of things."

"I like that," the Consultant said. "Less right. That is a great way to consider our next topic, *utilitarianism*, which is defined as the doctrine that an action is right insofar as it promotes happiness, and that the greatest happiness of the greatest number should be the guiding principle of conduct."[89]

"So, essentially," I said, "if a decision or particular action benefits the majority, it is deemed to be ethical, because a greater number benefits while a lesser number suffers, right?"

"Yes," he said. "In many ways, such thinking makes sense. After all, in a life-threatening situation, why should everyone die when only one person need give up his life for the benefit of the group, right? I suppose it's easy enough to justify such thinking as long as dying pertains to someone else." He gave a wry smile, and we all laughed.

"Utilitarianism is a monistic ethical theory with just one ultimate value, the maximization of happiness,"[90] he continued.

"In other words," a member from table respect said, "This theory is something of a balancing act where the end justifies the means. Correct?"

"Indeed," the Consultant said. "It incorporates collectivism as means for justifying behavior and deeming it 'ethical.' However, do you believe the notion of a greater good is itself ethically questionable if it violates ethical principles?"

"Absolutely," one of the detractors from the small group discussion said. "There's no way you can make an unethical choice and call it ethical."

"No one's calling it ethical!" a man retorted. "It's just a choice, and it's the better choice given the circumstances."

"Why isn't it ethical?" asked the Consultant.

"Because a greater good implies the existence of two levels of ethical behavior, and that one is preferred to another in a given circumstance," I said.

"Interesting," the Consultant replied as he stood behind the podium. He began, "There was a philosopher named Bentham who pondered this very question." He picked up a sheet of paper from the podium and read.

"Bentham's philosophy employs the notions of utility and hedonism in such a way as to provide a new foundation for making ethical judgments. As Frederick Copleston had written, 'Bentham did not invent the principle of utility: what he did was to expound and apply it explicitly and universally as the basic principle of both morals and legislation.' In this regard, Bentham was acting as a social reformer who sought to change the world. He vigorously attacked traditional morality and rejected notions of both the natural law and of natural human rights. Instead of approaching ethical philosophy in its traditional way, Bentham rested his theory solely upon the concept of psychological hedonism. That is, he used the observation from utility analysis that people seek pleasure and avoid pain as the basis upon which to devise a new moral standard of behavior. In essence, Bentham sought to make evil synonymous with pain and to make virtue synonymous with pleasure. This was his main point of departure from traditional ethics. Traditional moral philosophies tend to assert that virtuous actions will ultimately result in pleasure while evil actions will ultimately result in pain. But in traditional morality these things are never paired together as if they were one and the same thing. Rather, they exist together as causal pairs. This traditional approach to moral philosophy is readily espoused throughout the Bible as well. In fact, the traditional notion of wisdom is that the wise man is the one who prudently endures some immediate pain for a greater good. The main point of this is that Jonathan Edwards and the biblical writers never confused a person's pleasure with virtuous behavior itself, but rather saw it as a by-product of a life well-lived. Nevertheless, Bentham simply asserted that they are one and the same thing, and on this basis attempted to construct a new kind of moral guide.[91]

"Essentially, Bentham believed ethical behavior was anything that benefited the individual, or individuals, through the avoidance of pain and experience of pleasure, which he saw as opposite sides of the coin. What do you think about that?" he asked.

A young lady from table trust said, "I think that makes sense, but it doesn't come without a cost. I mean, you can't make a choice to save yourself at the expense of someone else and not pay a price. You have to live with yourself."

"Yeah," a man from table loyalty agreed. "Utilitarianism exists, I'm sure, and there are plenty of people who probably believe it, but I think, in the end, it's just a fancy term for people to justify behavior that others might find questionable. You know, 'I had no choice,' blah, blah, blah."

A few heads nodded. "Yes, but you do have a choice," a young girl from table honesty said. "You could make a *different* choice."

"That's crazy," a man shouted. "Who's going to sacrifice the group for the individual?"

"The individual, duh!" the young girl said.

"If the individual has the choice!" the man replied.

"So it's all about the group, and if the group decides their interest supersedes the interest of the individual, too bad? It kind of reminds me of *Lord of the Flies*. How is that good at all?"

"It's not that it's necessarily good," the Consultant chimed in. "The purpose of this discussion isn't to state utilitarianism is good. Utilitarianism is a theory based on Consequentialism, the right action is understood entirely in terms of consequences produced."[92]

"Right," the young girl continued. "And those consequences typically benefit the majority, or greater number of people, versus the minority, or less number of people. It sounds like group bullying to me."

"You are right," the Consultant said. "It places more value on the collective happiness and well-being of the group versus the individual and insinuates such happiness is for the *greater good* and is, therefore, more equal than the happiness of the individual. Did you notice that theme in the ethical dilemmas in your small group?"

Everyone nodded.

"In the ethical dilemma, *the Submarine Crew*, the apparent action is to drop the hatch and save the majority of people on the submarine by sacrificing the life of one crew member. Eighty-three percent of you believe dropping the hatch is the right thing to do in order to save more lives. So, apparently, the concept of a greater good has merit, don't you think?"

"It may have merit, especially on paper," a man from table compassion said, "but in those examples—and even in life, I suppose—a greater good isn't necessarily good at all if it means sacrifice for another human being."

His words hung in the air and we all thought about them for a moment.

"Ah," the Consultant said, "what your referring to is the element of guilt. Utilitarians often exhibit a level of guilt and conscientiousness about their own moral performance that belies the overt marginality of their commitment to the notion of moral duties."[93]

"What does that mean exactly?" a man from table compassion asked.

The Consultant surveyed the room and said, "Anyone?"

"I'll take a stab at it," I said. "I think it means that, although utilitarians believe in the concept of a greater good, they feel guilty about it. Perhaps because they realize that, like you said." I gestured at the man from table compassion. "Ultimately, their actions aren't completely ethical. While they may benefit the group and seem right, there is still an element of immorality in them."

"Very good," the Consultant said. "I couldn't have said it better myself." He turned and made his way back to the podium. "The idea that a greater good exists is present in all of us. We rationalize our behavior in order to justify a particular outcome that is favorable to us and less favorable to others. Many drape such actions in the blanket of fairness. However, as we have discussed, such decisions do not come freely. Individuals must bear the consequences of their actions." He paused as he glanced at his notes. "You have all made valid points, and this has been a terrific discussion. A great way to end our second day and a prelude to tomorrow's topic, moral standards."

And with that, he displayed a slide and assigned us to work on our daily leadership application and left the room.

> ## LEADERSHIP APPLICATION
>
> - What is the issue?
> - What are the implications for The Company?
> - Why does it matter?
> - How can The Company promote ethical behavior?
> - If ethical behavior increases, what would be the result?

Leadership Application

Again, we worked as a small group to answer the questions. We reviewed the day's topics, handouts, and small group discussion notes. Again, the receptionist recorded our answers.

1. The issue is that behavior—ethical and unethical—is often a reflection of values.
2. Unethical behavior is contagious. The Company needs ensure its practices are in keeping with ethical standards and its core values.
3. Once unethical behavior rears its ugly head, it can become commonplace and accepted practice and spread throughout the organization.

4. The Company can promote ethical behavior by punishing unethical behavior, rewarding ethical behavior, and conducting periodic training on ethics.
5. If there were an increase in ethical behavior, it would improve The Company's culture and the performance of its personnel.

I went back to my office. Like yesterday, the Consultant was waiting for me when I arrived.

"How did you enjoy today's training?" he asked.

"It was very eye-opening," I said as took my seat behind my desk. "A lot of very lively discussions."

"That's the idea," he said.

"Oh? And why is that?" I asked, genuinely interested.

"Lively discussion brings out a person's true character and allows you see how they really feel and what they truly believe," he said flatly.

Instead of checking his iPad as he had done yesterday, he asked me if I had been on the Company's Facebook or Twitter accounts today. I replied I hadn't, but the fact that he was asking was reason enough for me to login, which I did while he sat in silence. There were several new posts and dozens of comments about the training. One person wrote, "It's about time we had a forum to discuss some of the issues we see every day. Looking forward to tomorrow's topic, moral standards!" An employee who was not at the training commented, "Wow, it sounds like this training is really good. I sure hope I get to go, and it's not just for all the leaders."

I placed my fingers on the keyboard and was about to type when I thought better of it. The Consultant was watching me and asked what I was doing. When I told him, he said, "Why not respond, Cheryl? You're the CEO. Tell your employees this training is for everyone, and they will all have the opportunity to attend. I'm sure they'd love to hear it from you, the Company's leader." He smiled.

He was right. I replied to the post and continued to read what others were saying. Some posted comments about the topics from the group discussion, both large and small, which were really nothing more than a continuation of the day's discussions. I made a bold move and replied, "I just want everyone to know how much I am enjoying the discussions. I find the openness and honest dialogue very beneficial. Together, we can improve things at the Company."

Almost immediately, my post received several likes. I smiled. The Consultant noticed and asked why I was smiling, and I told him.

"That's good, Cheryl. It means your people are engaged in the process. They are flocking to social media to make their voices heard. Listen to them."

"I'm learning a lot, that's for sure," I said.

"Good. I'm very pleased to hear it." He rose, grabbed his bag, and said, "See you in the morning."

"Have a good night," I said.

After he left, I logged into Twitter and posted about the training. I noticed the Company hadn't made too many posts lately. *I'll have to check with PR about that,* I thought. I went back to Facebook and saw that my comment had twenty-two likes. There were two replies to my post. The first said, "I am enjoying the discussions too." The other said, "Do you think this training is really going to change things, change the people and the culture?" The post was from someone who wasn't at the training, but who obviously had been following the dialogue. I replied, "Training alone won't change things, but it's a start. I think you will enjoy the training and see the benefit." I probably sounded too much like the CEO and not a person, but I didn't want to start a public debate.

DAY 3
MORAL STANDARDS

Man must cease attributing his problems to his environment, and learn again to exercise his will—his personal responsibility in the realm of faith and morals.
—Albert Schweitzer

Defining Morals

The Consultant greeted everyone exuberantly. "Good morning, everyone. How are you enjoying the training so far?"

Comments were very positive and enthusiastic. Some people even said it was the best training the Company ever had. *I'll have to make a note of that,* I thought. It was good training.

I'm glad I ran into Robert at the deli. We spent the first ten minutes reviewing the topics from the previous day, and the Consultant reviewed the daily class climate assessments.

He took a moment to acknowledge a comment, which stated, "This is good training, but I don't think it's going to change anything." Rather than respond to the comment, he redirected it to the class and let us respond, which I thought was particularly effective. After all, this was our company, not his, so who better to provide input about the training and the Company? *What a concept*, I thought.

After several minutes of discussion, he continued, "Values, ethics, and morals all run together in most people's minds. However, as we have already discussed, values pertain to beliefs, both individually and collectively; and ethics pertain to right and wrong behavior based on values. Each are integral components of leadership (denominations, if you will) that function individually within the collective whole that make it effective—or not, as the case may be." He added with slight grin, "Today, we are going to build on those two concepts with a discussion about morals and morality." He paused to look down at his notes on the podium. "And we're going to discuss immorality too," he said with a wry smile as he displayed a slide.

MORAL STANDARDS

Day 3

He continued, "The term *moral* comes from the Latin word *moralis*, which has the same definition as the Greek word *ethos*, the custom or way of life.[94] Morals are concerned with the principles of right and wrong behavior and the goodness or badness of human character. They are a system of beliefs, typically with a religious or political foundation, that acts in tandem with one another within an established structure. Morals and the quality of being moral directly relates to human character, behavior, and the belief in the existence of right and wrong as it pertains to both individual and collective behavior. The term *moral* has been used to describe such things as *moral behavior, moral reasoning, moral equality, moral authority,* and *moral courage.* Its application to these terms is an attempt to define them in conjunction with a predetermined, and albeit absolute standard."

"So morals being a system of beliefs is essentially a collection of values?" a member from table loyalty asked.

"In a manner of speaking, yes," the Consultant said. "However, the concept of morality goes deeper than values."

"How so?" someone from table respect asked.

"Morals are closer to an absolute standard and don't change over the course of one's lifetime, like values."

"When you say 'absolute standard,' where does that originate?" asked a member from table compassion.

"The concept of morality can be traced back to the beginning of time. The first four chapters of the Bible, in the Book of Genesis, recount man's disobedience to God and the first murder in history when Cain killed his brother Abel. This was clearly immoral behavior."

"What about when Eve ate of the forbidden fruit?" I asked. "Wasn't that immoral?"

"No," he said. "It was disobedient but not immoral. Man's disobedience was wrong as compared to obedience, which was right. In regard to the account of Abel's murder by Cain's hand, a prominent theologian noted, 'It contains the first lie and the first human question in the Bible.'[95] He is referring to Genesis 4:9, in which Cain replies to God, 'I don't know. Am I my brother's keeper?' Although Adam and Eve had disobeyed God's command not to eat from the Tree of Knowledge of Good and Evil in the preceding chapters as was noted, Cain's behavior exceeds mere disobedience in that he *willfully* lied to God and questioned His authority to inquire his brother's whereabouts from him."

A young girl from table compassion asked, "Does that mean because there was a choice involved, the behavior was immoral, or does it mean the choice was the result of inner character, which in this case was immoral?"

"That is a great question," the Consultant responded, "And we will answer it in the remaining discussions throughout the day." He meandered around room.

He asked, "Does everyone believe the dividing line between right and wrong was clearly crossed by Adam and Eve, wrong being defined as disobedience?" Everyone nodded in concurrence. "So what is different about the story of Cain and Abel?"

A gentleman from table honesty said, "In Cain's case though, he not only disobeyed, he lied about his disobedience and then questioned God in regard to it! The boundaries of immorality expanded. And so the history of immoral behavior and its judgment continued throughout history."

"I couldn't have said it better myself," the Consultant said, beaming. "Morals are the manifestation of man's free will expressed by the choices he makes. In making moral choices, in rising above mere instinct, human beings transcend the realm of nature and enter a realm of freedom that belongs exclusively to them as rational creatures.[96] Morals, much like ethics, provide a standard by which behavior can be judged." He returned to the podium and read from his notes.

"Individuals are continually judging their own conduct and that of their fellows. They approve of some acts and call them 'right' or 'good.' They condemn other acts and call them 'wrong' or 'evil.' Moral judgments always have to do with the actions of human beings and, in particular, with voluntary actions—those actions freely chosen."[97]

A woman from my table said, "What I am getting from this is that morals differ from ethics in that ethics involve action based on values, and those values could be individual or collective. Furthermore, that behavior may not be true to one's character because of its collective component. But morality differs from ethical behavior because it's voluntary and without influence…instinctive almost, yes?"

The Consultant smiled. "That is an excellent observation. You are right on the money. Let me add to your comment. What is interesting to note from the quote I read is that morals serve as a dividing line between right and wrong and good and evil."

"So they distinguish and categorize behavior based on an inferred higher standard?" asked a man from table trust, somewhat skeptically. I got the distinct impression he did not believe in a higher authority.

"Essentially, yes," the Consultant said. "While the far corners of good and evil and right and wrong may in fact be distant from one another, only a thin line at their closest point of proximity separates them. Crossing the line between moral and immoral behavior can easily occur, if one is not cognizant of its location in regard to a particular situation and in relation to one's values."

A board member at table trust said, "The way I see it, morals differ from ethics in that ethics involve collective behavior based on values, whereas morals get their authority from something outside the individual—a higher being or higher authority (e.g., society)."[98]

"Yes," the Consultant said. "Morals are unique because they involve not only a collective reasoning; they involve a higher influence that can be religious, political, or social. In other words, ethics are the manifestation of individual values in a collective environment, whereas morals are values that are influence by a higher or greater authority than ourselves."

He read from a document. "For example, if society is dominated by a single religious or cultural belief system, as is the case in some countries, then what is ethical and what is moral may be defined as the same thing. In societies where there is no monolithic belief system, there can be very wide differences in opinion in society as to whether a given action is ethical or moral."[99]

He looked up. "What are your thoughts about that?"

"We used to have a somewhat singular belief system in this country, although, I wouldn't necessarily call it monolithic," I commented. "But we have become incredibly diverse in the past several decades. As a result, I'd say there is disparity between what is considered ethical and what is considered moral."

He nodded.

A woman, who was a bit rough around the edges at an adjacent table, spoke. "I've seen a lot [of] unethical and immoral behavior here at the Company, particularly in the past year," she said, glancing in my direction. *What was she implying?* I wondered. "I'll just go ahead and put it out there. A lot of you heard what happened at the Company picnic, the drinking and skinny-dipping…,"

"I don't think that is something we need to discuss," a member of the board said bitterly. "The problem was handled, and the individuals involved were disciplined."

"Disciplined?" she protested. "What does that mean? Their behavior was swept under the table because they were senior managers."

"That's enough!" he said, pointing his finger and raising his voice.

The consultant intervened. "Okay, let's discuss this calmly in light of our topic." He looked over at the woman. "Did you bring this up because you believe the behavior was immoral in some way?"

"I brought it up because I believe their behavior was inappropriate, unethical, and immoral—not to mention, the company's lack of a real response." She glared at the board member. *Well, this was certainly getting interesting,* I thought. *I knew about the incident in question, and I knew the people involved had received memos on the record in their personnel files. One individual, though, a junior employee had been terminated. Was there something to her argument,* I wondered.

"What I'd like to know," she continued, "based on what you just read, is how anyone can consider their behavior to be anything but immoral."

A man from a table across the room said, "I'll give you that it was unethical, but saying that it was immoral involves judging their behavior based on a higher standard, and I just don't know that a higher standard applies in this situation."

"How can it not?" she asked.

"There's no absolute when it comes to skinny-dipping," he said.

"Well, maybe there isn't, but there's an absolute when it comes to personal conduct," she retorted. "So to me, it was immoral. It shouldn't have happened, and it was wrong."

"Okay," the Consultant said. He looked over at the board member, who was very obviously trying to contain his indignation at the discussion of the issue. "You both make valid points. Morals very much involve what is often referred to as *human nature*. That is, not only who and what we are, but also who and what we ought to be.[100] In other words, *know thyself*. In fact, Aristotle believed knowing oneself was a combination of knowing one's competence (what a person can do) and character (who a person invariably is)."[101]

"What you're saying," a member of table loyalty said, "is the concept of morality is greater than ourselves and deeply engrained in psychological application. Correct?"

"Yes," the Consultant said. "Let me read you an excerpt from a recent article in *the New York Times*."

"Morality is not just any old topic in psychology but close to our conception of the meaning of life. Moral goodness is what gives each of us the sense that we are worthy human beings. We seek it in our friends and mates, nurture it in our children, advance it in our politics, and justify it with our religions. A disrespect for morality is blamed for everyday sins and history's worst atrocities. To carry this weight, the concept of morality would have to be bigger than any of us and outside all of us."[102]

He looked up from the article and surveyed the room. "What are your thoughts about that?"

"What the article is saying," I said, "is that we seek goodness in ourselves and others in order to establish a common sense of worth. At least that's how I take it."

"You are right on track," the Consultant said. "Other thoughts?"

A young woman from table respect said, "I think it goes deeper than that. How do you explain the atrocities it mentions? Does it mean those committing them are immoral as it relates to an absolute standard, or do they believe they are acting morally in conjunction with their beliefs?"

"So what you're asking is," the Consultant summarized, "are some actions and behavior immoral regardless of one's beliefs?"

"Yes," she said.

"Any takers?" he asked as he scanned the room.

"I'll give it a go," a man from table compassion said. "To acknowledge morality is really to acknowledge the existence of a higher power, the awareness of which is innate to all of us. Immoral behavior, therefore, is the rejection of that idea."

"Very good," the Consultant said. "There are many theories as to the origin of man's moral awareness and resulting behavior and judgment. However, scientists and psychologists have not yet determined a definitive explanation for its origin. What is interesting to note is," he said as he read from a document, "moral judgment is pretty consistent from person to person, says Marc Hauser, professor of psychology at Harvard University and author of *Moral Minds*. Moral behavior, however, is scattered all over the chart. The rules we know, even the ones we intuitively feel, are, by no means, the rules we always follow.[103]

We are preprogrammed for moral behavior—or so it seems. Cicero believed that all human beings possessed 'certain seeds,' which, if nurtured, would enable one to develop moral virtue.[104] From this, individuals develop character, which can have quite a magnetic effect on others."

It was time for our morning break before heading into our small groups. Our topic was character. *This was going to be interesting*, I thought.

Character

"Okay," the shipping clerk said, "we are going to discuss character." He thumbed through the folder provided by the Consultant and extracted a document. "'The word *character*," he said, "'is derived from the Greek word *charattein*, meaning to engrave."[105] He paused and looked up from his paper.

"I suppose, that means who we are ultimately is engrained in us, or rather engraved in us, according to the Greek," I said. "Sort of like a fingerprint."

"That might be true to a certain extent," the facilities manager said. "But do you think character is as permanent as a fingerprint or is it subject to change, based on values and the situation?"

"Who you are is who you are," interjected the receptionist. "That doesn't really change."

"Sure, it does," the account executive said. "We're all influenced by our environments, people, and life in general. Experiences mold our character over time." He looked at the shipping clerk, who was skimming his document. "What does the file say about character?"

"It says character is often associated with one's moral virtue, which is the strengths that make it possible for human beings to pursue uniquely human aims or goods successfully."[106]

"Meaning, moral virtue is based on the idea that man is predisposed to know right from wrong and understands the difference between good and evil and makes appropriate choices, right?" asked the account executive.

"So it would seem," I said. "And those choices then determine and individual's character."

"Yes," the shipping clerk continued excitedly as he read, "Cicero believed character was comprised of four interactions."

1. People are endowed alike with the gift of reason and hence an innate regard of the 'good' and the four cardinal virtues (wisdom, justice, courage, moderation).
2. The assignment of various qualities or aptitudes: mental, physical, emotional, etc.
3. The result of external circumstances or chance such as a person's upbringing or social economic background.
4. Choice: the type of person an individual strives to be.[107]

"So," the Receptionist said, "it would appear character—and correspondingly, moral virtue—is thus an amalgam of nature, choice, and environment."

"Yes," I said. "This combination of factors essentially determines the direction of our moral compass, or as you alluded to earlier, who we are."

The shipping clerk continued to read from the folder. "In regard to character, Lord Moran stated that character is a habit, the choice of right instead of wrong; it is a moral quality, which grows to maturity in peace and is not suddenly developed on the outbreak of war. For war, in spite of what we have heard to the contrary, has no power to transform. It merely exaggerates the good and evil that is in us, till it is plain for all to read. It cannot change, it exposes. Man's fate in battle is worked out before war begins."[108]

"You see," the receptionist beamed, "he agrees with me. Lord Moran was stating that an individual's character is innate and cannot be truly witnessed, except through external circumstances and that those circumstances do not necessarily change one's character as much as magnify it. We are who we are. Period!"

"I disagree," the facilities manager said. "Sure we are who we are, but we are capable of change. It's not as though our character is imbedded in our DNA and cannot change. It grows and develops."

"I'm with you," the account executive said, pointing at the facilities manager. "People act out of character once and a while, due to unforeseen circumstances."

"I suppose you are right," the shipping clerk said snidely. *What's going on here?* I wondered. Everyone had grown eerily quiet.

"What's on your mind?" the account executive asked.

The shipping clerk hesitated. Finally, he said, "Oh, I was just thinking about the Company's picnic a few months ago."

"What about it?" I asked.

"Well, we all know what happened. Let's face it. I doubt there's anyone in the Company who didn't hear about the drinking and skinny-dipping. It was the talk of the Company for days."

"And?" I prompted.

"Well, is what happened that day indicative of those individual's true character or was it simply a matter of 'acting out of character,' as you said?" He motioned to the account executive. "How do we make that distinction, especially when it comes to leadership?"

"I'll take this one," I said, glancing at the account manager and facilities manager. "Leaders must be men and women whose character is morally intact. A leader's character must be grounded on such core values as integrity, trust, truth, and human dignity, which influence the leader's vision, ethics, and behavior.[109] Character is built on the foundation of values. It identifies a leader's moral qualities immediately through actions, behavior, and personal interactions with others."

"I agree," he said. "So what happened that day? Where was their integrity? I think those of who were there witnessed firsthand just *who those individuals really were!*"

"Well," I said, "in certain sense, you're right. Character manifests itself at all times, but particularly during times of adversity and challenge, which are apt to bring an individual's true nature to the surface. As such, character is a leader's moral center.[110] It is his or her essence, the person one sees in the mirror."

Our time was passing quickly, and the shipping clerk fumbled through the folder, making sure he had covered everything. He pulled an article fro the folder and said, "An article in *Forbes* observed that character is comprised of the following attributes:

1. Integrity—people who are deeply aware of themselves in relation to others. It is the moral or virtuous sense, a defining characteristic.
2. Trustworthiness—a true leader can be trusted to do the right thing. It cannot be learned; it's innate.
3. Emotional intelligence—an awareness of others.
4. Openness—open to ideas, people, risk, challenge, opportunity and experience. This requires and open mind and open heart.
5. Motivation—lead by example, possess infectious energy, and fundamental accountability."[111]

"Yes," the account executive said. "I've been in the business world for decades, and I can tell you, these attributes combine to form an individual's moral fingerprint and become the quintessence of his or her character. Like values, character fundamentally shapes how we engage the world around us, what we notice, what we reinforce, who we engage in conversation, what we value, what we choose to act on, how we decide—and the list goes on."[112]

"I agree," I said. "Defining character is more about identifying its components than stating a definition. I think we all have an idea of what character is, but trying to spell it for every person is nearly impossible, given our differences as people."

The shipping clerk passed out copies of a diagram. "This sheet (figure 3) illustrates the various components that contribute to character development," he said.

We all studied the diagram in silence.

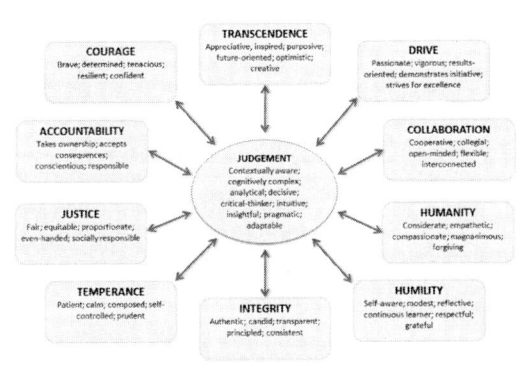

Figure 3 — Character components centered on JUDGEMENT (Contextually aware; cognitively complex; analytical; decisive; critical-thinker; intuitive; insightful; pragmatic; adaptable), surrounded by:

- **COURAGE**: Brave; determined; tenacious; resilient; confident
- **TRANSCENDENCE**: Appreciative, inspired; purposive; future-oriented; optimistic; creative
- **DRIVE**: Passionate; vigorous; results-oriented; demonstrates initiative; strives for excellence
- **ACCOUNTABILITY**: Takes ownership; accepts consequences; conscientious; responsible
- **COLLABORATION**: Cooperative; collegial; open-minded; flexible; interconnected
- **JUSTICE**: Fair; equitable; proportionate; even-handed; socially responsible
- **HUMANITY**: Considerate; empathetic; compassionate; magnanimous; forgiving
- **TEMPERANCE**: Patient; calm; composed; self-controlled; prudent
- **INTEGRITY**: Authentic; candid; transparent; principled; consistent
- **HUMILITY**: Self-aware; modest; reflective; continuous learner; respectful; grateful

Figure 3

Finally, the shipping clerk read, "In regard to these attributes, professors Crossan, Gandz, and Seijts observed that character is not something that you have or don't have. All of us have character, but the key is the depth of development of each facet of character that enables us to lead in a holistic way. Character is not a light switch that can be turned on and off. There are degrees, and every situation presents a different experience and opportunity to learn and deepen character."[113]

"Indeed," I said, "our character is always *on* for others to observe. Therefore, it serves as an individual's moral shadow cast in the light of circumstance." I smiled knowingly, hoping everyone would take my meaning in light of the reference to the picnic incident. It must have worked, because no one had any comments.

We all went to lunch together again. I had to admit, I was really enjoying the camaraderie and conversation over lunch each day.

Moral Behavior and the Law

"So," the Consultant said, "how was your morning small group? I heard some lively discussions as I walked past the conference rooms." He smiled. *He seems to be enjoying this*, I thought. He spent a few minutes reviewing the concept of character with the group.

"Nothing to see here," one man quipped humorously." We all laughed.

"Well," he said, "I'm delighted everyone is having such a good time. Are you all learning a few things?"

Everyone nodded. A few uh-huhs rang out along with some Oh, yeahs.

"Splendid," he said. "I'm glad to hear that since we are going to continue our discussion about morals. When many people consider moral behavior, they cannot help but think about the law, right and wrong, as it pertains to the actions of others within the confines of society. In particular, I immediately think of the Ten Commandments found in the Bible in the book of Exodus chapter twenty."

He displayed a slide and read through them one at a time.

TEN COMMANDMENTS

You shall have no other gods before me.

You shall not make for yourself an image in the form of anything in heaven above or on the earth beneath or in the waters below. You shall not bow down to them or worship them; for I, the Lord your God, am a jealous God, punishing the children for the sin of the parents to the third and fourth generation of those who hate me, but showing love to a thousand generations of those who love me and keep my commandments.

You shall not misuse the name of the Lord your God, for the Lord will not hold anyone guiltless who misuses his name.

> ## TEN COMMANDMENTS
>
> Remember the Sabbath day by keeping it holy. Six days you shall labor and do all your work, but the seventh day is a Sabbath to the Lord your God. On it you shall not do any work, neither you, nor your son or daughter, nor your male or female servant, nor your animals, nor any foreigner residing in your towns. For in six days the Lord made the heavens and the earth, the sea, and all that is in them, but he rested on the seventh day. Therefore the Lord blessed the Sabbath day and made it holy.
>
> Honor your father and your mother, so that you may live long in the land the Lord your God is giving you.

> ## TEN COMMANDMENTS
>
> You shall not murder.
>
> You shall not commit adultery.
>
> You shall not steal.
>
> You shall not give false testimony against your neighbor.
>
> You shall not covet your neighbor's house. You shall not covet your neighbor's wife, or his male or female servant, his ox or donkey, or anything that belongs to your neighbor."

He glanced up as he began to walk around the room. "These Commandments are concise and provide a standard of behavior that is based on God's values, not man's. As such, they are the historical basis for moral behavior and are equally applicable to all cultures and nationalities without bias or prejudice, which is why we are going to study them."

"That's a little risqué, isn't it?" asked a young girl from table respect.

"Perhaps," he said. "However, the historical relevance and moral content of the Ten Commandments can be studied independently of religious proselytizing. I'm not here to preach to anyone," he said with a quick smile. "So do you believe the Ten Commandments are applicable today, or are they simply antiquated concepts from prehistoric times?"

"Of course, they are still applicable," a gentleman from table honesty said. "They're timeless. They apply to everyone on this planet."

"I don't know if I'd go that far," a young woman from table trust said. "You believe they apply to everyone on the planet?"

"How can they not?" he asked. "Which ones don't you think apply to everyone?"

"Well, what about adultery? Not everyone believes in marriage or monogamy, so that might not apply," she retorted.

"What?" a lady at her table said glaring at her. "You think adultery is acceptable?"

"I didn't say that," she denied. "I'm only citing that as a possible example."

"I think that's a bad example!" she practically shouted. *Hmm. I wonder what's going on there. Perhaps that comment hit too close to home.*

"Okay, fine, whatever. How about having no other gods before me? Not everyone believes in God, ya know."

"Okay," she said. "I'll go a long with that one."

"Well," a man from table compassion said, "if that holds true, then a few others might not apply either."

"This is very good," the Consultant said. He was genuinely pleased to have stirred the pot so vigorously. "When it comes to the Ten Commandments," he continued as he read from a document at the podium, "Rudolf Steiner argued that the Ten Commandments are more extensive and general than the laws of any modern state and have validity independent of their time and place. He further suggested that the Ten Commandments are held to be universal and people are conscious of them as having the same effect as any modern legislature. Adherents to the three religions in this study: Christianity, Judaism, and Islam are committed to the Ten Commandments as moral and *ethical* [emphasis mine] guidelines."[114]

He looked up. "Do you think that's true? Do you believe the Ten Commandments are more expansive and inclusive than our modern laws?"

"Absolutely," a man at table respect said. "If you think about it, they pretty much provide a standard of behavior for everyone that if we all followed, or tried to follow, would negate the need for modern laws."

"I don't know about that," a woman from table honesty said. "Those were simpler times. What about things like drugs? I don't see how the Ten Commandments apply to drugs."

"Nothing specifically, but someone who does drugs might consider them their god, or they could become a god of sort," a man at my table said. *That was an interesting interpretation,* I thought. *I liked it.*

"What is interesting to consider," the Consultant interjected, "is over two thousand years ago, moral behavior was an issue that necessitated a standard. In this particular case, God provided the standard that many believe still holds true today. Students of business ethics and management agree that the Ten Commandments provide the moral foundation for both individuals and groups, and that the Ten Commandments should be regarded as general moral guidelines for personal and business conduct."[115]

A gentlemen from table compassion said, "The Ten Commandments have come under heavy scrutiny and criticism over the past few decades, mostly due to the belief that a public display violates constitutional rights."[116]

"You're right," the Consultant said. "What is fascinating about this issue is the placement of the Ten Commandments in public schools, state capitals, and courthouses. An ancient standard, considered by some to be an anachronism, was still relevant and applicable to a modern society. This coincides with academic research that stipulates moral standards are transcendent across cultures and throughout history; they are universally applicable and timeless."

He paused and surveyed the room. "What about modern law and the Ten Commandments?"

"Modern law is a reflection of the sentiment contained in the Ten Commandments, which concisely spell out what constitutes acceptable behavior," a gentleman at table compassion said. He continued, "At a minimum, the law prescribes and proscribes morally laden behaviors, but it also unabashedly attempts to shape moral attitudes and beliefs. When the law forbids murder, we know that this is because the law has decided that murder is evil and wishes all citizens to agree with that assessment."[117]

"Excellent!" the Consultant said. "The law is very closely linked to morality and upholds general moral standards within the confines of society. In essence, the law engages in moral regulation even where it cannot plausibly be aiming to change behaviors, attitudes, or emotions; the law simply expresses moral commitments shared (often very controversially) by the polity at large.[118] The law is a representative moral consensus, not a universal standard. The law does not regulate morals or morality."

He returned to podium and reviewed his notes. "A law changes 'morality' when it (a) changes a person's behavior or attitudes, by (b) changing how the person believes they and others 'ought' to behave or think."[119]

"That's true," a man at table loyalty said. "Simply enacting a law, or changing a law, does not change people's behavior. You don't change people by passing the laws and forcing them to [comply]. That's a great mistake we make. What you need is a consensus among the people [that a particular behavior is wrong,] and the laws kind of follow along after that."[120]

"Your point is well taken," the Consultant said. "Therefore, the law is the expressed collective moral opinion of the majority. However, because of the diverse nature of society, the law is perhaps a particularly powerful source for shaping and sustaining moral norms, because the law is a common denominator for all citizens."[121]

A board member from the adjacent table said, "Perhaps more important than the content of the law is the perception of the law. That is, the law must be perceived to be equitable, authoritative, expert, and trustworthy in order to effectively regulate moral behavior. The law is a reflection of dominant perception. Thus, changing laws reflect popular opinion and a shift in moral behavior."

"Terrific!" the Consultant exclaimed. "How ironic you mention shifting morality. We are going to discuss that later this afternoon. Something to remember about the law, though, is the law can shape moral behaviors by simply shifting the costs and benefits of the activity being regulated. However, it is more interesting, and more helpful to a governing regime, when law changes people's moral response to regulated activities, making citizens more or less likely to engage in the behavior without the need for direct enforcement."[122]

"So what you're saying," a member from my table said, "is the law serves the people best, not by enforcing standards via consequences, but by influencing the will of the people to act in a manner that is socially acceptable and morally responsible. In effect, the law acts as a dividing line, a barrier, between what is deemed *right* and *wrong*. The responsibility to act morally and behave properly lies with the people, who must be cognizant of the law's presence and ramifications."

"Yes," the Consultant said. "The law serves as a warning of consequences that could be imposed if violated and provides a socially universal moral standard beneficial to the common good of the people." He looked down at the podium and picked up a document. "Let me conclude our morning session by quoting. Thomas Aquinas argued that genuine law has four essential characteristics; Law, he says, is 'nothing else than an ordinance of reason for the common good, made by him who has care of the community, and promulgated.' In other words, Thomas argues first that genuine law is rational, something that the mind grasps as right; second, that it necessarily is for the common good rather than the good of a select few; third, that it must be initiated by the person or persons authorized to initiate it; and fourth, that it must be promulgated, announced, made known to those toward whom it is directed. And this is characteristic of all law, not merely the natural law."[123]

I said, "So the law is an implemented method of moral codes and standards designed to protect and benefit all citizens equally, right?"

"Yes. It is also a reflection of moral authority."

It was time for our break and time to head to the conference room for our afternoon small group. It was my turn in the rotation, so I stayed behind to be briefed with the other small group leaders.

Natural Law, Moral Authority, and Responsibility

Our small group topic was natural law. *This should be good*, I mused. *And I'm the lucky one stuck with this topic.*

I removed the documents from the small group folder and skimmed them. "Okay, everyone," I said. "I'm back for another round." Everyone smiled. I read, "Moral authority is often referred to as *natural law*, which is that there are certain foundational principles of morality that are the same…both as to knowledge and to rectitude…principles of morality that are not only right for all human beings but knowable (and at some level known) to all human beings."[124]

"So natural law stems from a higher power, right?" asked the shipping clerk.

"Yes," I said.

"It doesn't have to be from a higher power," the account executive said. "It can simply be known through nature."

"But doesn't nature imply a creator, and, thus, a higher power?" asked the facilities manager. "Or are we going to assume nature simply exists?"

"I guess it depends on one's beliefs about creation and a creator," the account executive said. "For some, nature exists separately from a creator." the facilities manager nodded.

I looked down at the folder and read, "The *Encyclopedia Britannica* defines natural law as a system of right or justice held to be common to all humans and derived from nature rather than from the rules of society, or positive law."

"In other words," the account executive said, "the source of natural law can be found in nature, which, according to many proponents of natural law, was created by God."

"I agree," the receptionist said. "It is discoverable and easily known by everyone. As such, it is universal and equally applicable, regardless of culture or nationality. However, it doesn't necessarily need to be attributed to God, especially if someone doesn't believe in God."

"Right," I said. "However, natural law implies the existence of an absolute standard when it comes to right and wrong—namely God, or other supreme being—even though there are many who deny his existence or the existence of a supreme authority."

"I suppose that's why the term *natural law* is used," the facilities manager said as he smiled. "It's politically correct."

The receptionist jumped on that. "I disagree. Natural law is *not* a substitute for God. It's merely the admission or recognition of nature's laws, and laws that are universally applicable."

She's pretty adamant about that, I thought.

I reviewed the material in the folder before commenting. I read, "Natural law is higher and absolutely valid and just, because it emanates from the will of God. The will of God is—in the natural law doctrine—identical to nature, insofar as nature is conceived of as created by God, and the law of nature is an expression of God's will. Because of its divine character, natural law is absolutely binding and overrules all other laws."[125]

"So natural law is just a fancy way of saying God's will, right?" asked the shipping clerk.

"I think it's a bit more complex than that," the account executive interjected. "I think natural law is the expression of how things are supposed to be according to God's plan—for those who recognize him, that is. His will and his plan are contained in nature as evidence of his existence, but natural law extends beyond his will. It affects, or should affect, how we behave and conduct ourselves."

"Okay," I said. "Do you think natural law is superior to the law?"

"What law would that be?" the account executive asked. "Man's law?"

"Yes," I answered.

"That's hard to say," the receptionist said. "Laws are important, and like we discussed earlier, the law is a reflection of morality. So doesn't it stand to reason that the law is just as important as natural law?"

"Not necessarily," the facilities manager said. "Man's laws serve his needs, whereas natural law serves God's will. If we accept that natural law is a reflection of God and God is perfect, then our laws—no matter how well intended and right they may seem—are inferior to natural law in some manner."

"Right," the account executive said. "Our laws are good, and they may even support natural law, but in the end, natural law is the standard from which our laws are derived."

"What about atheists?" asked the receptionist. "Some people don't believe in God. Therefore, they would deny the existence of natural law."

"Would they?" asked the facilities manager. "They might deny the existence of God, but they might recognize the presence of natural law in nature."

As interesting as this conversation was, I didn't want the group to go down that rabbit hole, or we'd never finish our assignment. The Consultant had warned us about going too far off topic when he gave the group leaders their instructions.

"Okay," I said, interrupting. "Great points all around. Let's stay on track before we veer too far off course. Natural law is the backbone of many religions. Christianity, in particular, traces the rule of law back to the Old Testament. Even before God gave the law to His people, there was a sense of natural law, of right and wrong, in the opening chapters of Genesis. Natural law is the moral revelation that God gives in creation itself,"[126] I read from the folder. "I believe that's what we were just saying."

"Yes," the facilities manager said. "Supporters of natural law, like me, contend that God has made His presence known through the majesty of creation. 'Natural revelation means what it sounds like, namely, the revelation of God in nature. It is sometimes called *general revelation*, because it is available to everybody.'"[127]

"True," the account executive said. "Although discoverable through nature, adhering to natural law is difficult, because natural law obliges us to do the straight thing regardless of the pain, danger, or difficulty involved. Natural Law is hard—as hard as nails,[128] as they say."

The receptionist added, "Evidence of natural law's existence is based on the laws of nature. According to some, the presence of particular laws in nature and their relationship to creation is indicative of a higher authority to which one must ascribe."

"Yes," the shipping clerk said. "Such laws are distinct and disparate from man-made laws."

I removed copies of a quote from the folder and passed them around the table. We all read in silence.

> Under equal conditions, things that are equal behave in the same way—at all times and in all places. This is often taken as a logical basis—the principle of identity—for all laws of Nature. It is generally based on experience—though this is not absolutely required. These laws of Nature are established by things and their relations with one another. They are quantifiable. Christian Wolff calls them 'mensurabiles.' Quantifiability is regarded as a prerequisite for a natural relationship to be susceptible to formulation as a law with any certainty, security and consistency. Mathematics represents their application. The laws of nature are impersonal, and this crucially distinguishes them from man-made laws. With this in mind, Hegel differentiated between 'Laws of Nature and Laws of Right' (Rechtsgesetze). 'The Laws of Nature quite simply exist, and apply as they are: they do not suffer degeneration … The criteria for these laws lie outside us.' 'Rechtsgesetze,' on the other hand, are 'made'—usually manmade—and are not absolute. 'Positive jurisprudence' therefore 'often has to deal only with contradictions.' The concept of the man-made law ('Rechtsgesetz') is central to all consolidated social systems and at the same time is

> a prerequisite for any attempt to create 'systematic' scientific disciplines. A 'Rechtsgesetz' aims to lay down obligations, and 'describe what should happen.' It is created by human beings and focuses above all on their actions and behavior, but also on the ordering of things and regulation of matters. It has to take into account its anthropological determination in terms of those who are subject to it and its chronological determination in terms of the matters it regulates.[129]

"I think what this is saying," the account executive said, "is in essence, natural law simply exists. It is independent of man and out of his control. The laws of nature are a prime example. Man has no control over gravity, yet he is bound by it. The same is true of natural law."

"True," I said. "Man has established laws in order to regulate and quantify behavior, but these laws are separate from natural law and exist within the control of man. Natural law is external to man and is beyond his control."

"So natural law is based on *moral authority*. That is, authority beyond the law, a higher standard, right?" asked the shipping clerk.

"Yes," the facilities manager said. "For religious folks, moral authority is an inherent right given by God. It requires adherence, because one will be held accountable. As such, one must act accordingly and exhibit exemplary conduct."

"In other words," the receptionist said, "moral authority is something we should all recognize or be able to decipher in nature, right?"

"Yes," the account executive said. "Moral authority accessible by reason is referred to as the natural law written on the hearts of all men and women, a term which draws upon St. Paul's letter to the Romans." He removed a small copy of the New Testament from his jacket pocket and thumbed to a particular page. He read, "When gentiles who have not the law do by nature what the law requires, they are a law to themselves. They show that what the law requires is written on their hearts" (Rom. 2:14–15, NIV).[130] He replaced the book back in his pocket.

I glanced at my watch. We were just about out of time. I checked the folder to make sure I had hit all the required points. In summary, I said, "Moral authority, a.k.a. natural law, places moral requirements on everyone regardless of culture, nationality, geographic location, or man-made law. It mandates people act in a prescribed manner, because the moral standard is pre-programmed in all of us. Thus, we have a moral responsibility to obey and act accordingly. Moral responsibility is an obligation to our fellow man and ourselves to uphold the internal standard provided by our Creator. It necessitates doing the *right* thing."

We finished up, gathered our things, and headed back to the training room for our last group discussion of the day.

The New Morality

"Good afternoon, everyone," the Consulted greeted. "I hope you enjoyed your small group session on morals and natural law. This afternoon, we are going to push the envelope, in a manner of speaking. We are going to discuss the new morality. That is, a shift in moral alignment that has occurred over the past several decades." He began to wander around the room. "So," he continued, "do you believe morality changes?"

What a loaded question, I thought.

An older gentleman from table honesty replied, "No, I don't believe morality changes. I believe society changes in regard to it."

"How so?" the Consultant asked.

"Well," he answered, "I believe that as a society, we change how we interpret and apply moral standards in order to suit our needs."

"Can you cite an example?" the Consultant asked.

"Well, just recently, some states changed their laws on marijuana use. Marijuana is legal, in at least some form, in twenty-two states and in the District of Columbia. Most allow it for medical use only. Colorado and Washington, this year, enacted laws that allow recreational use by adults."[131]

"So legalizing marijuana represents a shift in morality?" the Consultant asked.

"Sure," he said.

"I disagree," a young man from table compassion said, somewhat defiantly. "Marijuana has a lot of medical benefits. The only difference between it and medications produced by the big pharmaceutical companies is that it doesn't generate billions in revenue!"

"That's not true," the older gentleman protested. "Marijuana might have some medicinal benefits. I won't argue that. But using it shouldn't be legalized, just so people can get high and feel good."

"Why not? Alcohol is legal," he retorted.

The Consultant simply stood in the center of the room and observed the dialogue exchange. I honestly think he was amused.

"You both make excellent points," he said. "I hate to intrude, but we must continue. We'll come back to your points shortly. Okay, that is one example of a possible shift in morality. Can anyone think of another?"

"How about marriage?" a woman from table respect said. "I had a conversation with my teenage daughter about marriage, and she told me the concept of marriage was outdated."

Wow! That's interesting, I thought. I guess I am a bit old-fashioned in my thinking.

"Outdated?" the Consultant asked.

"Yes. She told me no one gets married anymore and said more Americans are living together without getting married, and some are raising families, just without the gold bands."[132]

"Okay," the Consultant said as he navigated the conversation. "Is marriage a moral issue?" he asked as he made his way back to the podium.

"I believe it is," a board member from table loyalty said. "As we've studied this week, culture plays a significant role in the formation of values, ethical behavior, and morality. Marriage is a social institution that has defined the concept of family for centuries. As marriage and society have declined, so has the morality."

"Very interesting," the Consultant said, as he picked up the remote from the podium. "I was hoping we'd hit the topic of marriage. I read an article that lists the top five reasons millennials aren't marrying."

He displayed a slide on the screen.

TOP FIVE REASONS

1. Driven by career
2. True love isn't waiting
3. Men are acting like boys
4. They don't know how to date
5. Singleness is attractive

Carrie Mitchell, "5 Reasons Religious Millennials Aren't Marrying," Faithstreet.com (April 8, 2014)

We all read through them. I couldn't help but smirk a little at number three. I'd like to read that article and learn a bit more. "Are millennials immoral because they don't view marriage positively?" he asked. "Or have they been impacted by technology and a cultural shift?"

"I don't think the answer is as simple as that," a woman at table honesty said. "Sure, technology has impacted society. Dating isn't what is used to be. Young people would rather text and e-mail than have a conversation. But that alone isn't the answer."

"True," I said. "But technology has impacted everything, so it only seems natural that it would impact how society perceives morality."

"Yes," said a man from my table, "but do you think morality has changed, or has our interpretation of morality changed?"

"Oh, I believe our perception of morality has changed. Based on what we covered today, morality is as close to an absolute standard as we can get. What's changed is how we interpret and apply morality," I said.

"Ah," he said. "We apply morality! I like that. Indeed we do. Let me read you something." He retrieved a document from the podium.

"An unprecedented values shift has swept into American society since the 1960s: People have begun go make moral decisions based on their own needs rather than deferring to traditional religious and governmental sources of authority.

Never have so many people been so free of moral constraint as contemporary Americans. As people demand the right to decide ethical and spiritual issues on their own terms, they are redefining the social context for moral decision-making. A world of restraint is being replaced by a world of possibility. Social order has depended upon the willingness of people to follow their conscience, not their desires. That era is fading."[133]

When he finished, he asked, "Do you agree? Are we redefining the social context for moral decision-making?"

"I think so," a member from table trust said. "We've gotten away from traditional values and are redefining morality as we see it."

"What do you mean by 'traditional values'?" he asked.

"I mean the right to life, fidelity in marriage, marriage between one man and one woman, and religious freedom.[134] You know, all the things that have fallen under attack in the past decade or so."

The Consultant gave a brief smile. "So you believe traditional values are representative of morality?"

"Yes," he said. "Absolutely."

"I disagree," a young girl said, somewhat vehemently. "I think traditional values are based on antiquated ideas. They don't leave room for change. Cavemen used to drag their women back to their caves by their hair, and that was considered moral or the right thing to do, because that's how things were then."

"It may have been the accepted practice," the member from table trust responded, "but that doesn't mean it was right. Just because things are changing today, doesn't make it right. Like he read,"—he pointed at the Consultant—"we're redefining the social context in which we apply morals. That doesn't change the morals themselves, just the application and interpretation."

She persisted. "Morality is not a constant. What a group of people finds to be morally acceptable or morally unacceptable evolves over time, generally, because of an increased understanding or awareness, and generally, this occurs (we like to think) in a more progressive, positive direction."[135]

He shot back, "You think the way society is going is morally correct? You don't believe our moral compass is pointing the wrong way?"

Just as she was ready to respond, the Consultant intervened. "This has been very stimulating. We could go on for hours. However, our time is just about up, so let me conclude by reading you something." He was behind the podium looking down as he read. "Consider this," he said. "Americans today want to hear moral second opinions as they make up their minds about various issues. Such independent thinking is beginning to change institutions that have been accustomed to wielding moral authority. In a time of moral freedom, no institution will be able to stick its head in the sand and pretend that people can approach it for advice, and guidance can be treated as supplicants. The twenty-first century will be the century of moral freedom."[136]

He paused for moment and said, "The currency of leadership must be moral or it will have little or no value." With that, he displayed a slide on the screen, instructed us to complete our leadership application, gathered his things, and exited the room.

> ## LEADERSHIP APPLICATION
>
> - What is the issue?
> - What are the implications for The Company?
> - Why does it matter?
> - How can The Company promote moral conduct?
> - If morality increases, what would be the result?

Leadership Application

We were accustomed to the routine and wanted to answer the questions as quickly as possible, since it was Wednesday. The past three days had been fun, but they were taxing too. Plus, I knew the Consultant would be waiting in my office when we finished. We all agreed somewhat that morality was a constant, and the only thing that really changed was our application and interpretation of it. As we saw it, the issue for the Company was the way in which employees applied morality. If we kept going the way we were, everyone was going to have a field day, which meant my days and the Company's were numbered.

Aside from training like this, we came up with the idea to develop a set of morals for the Company and post them prominently. Additionally, they would be reinforced through semi-annual training. One person had the idea to create the *morality committee*, a committee that would design, develop, and implement events and campaigns throughout the year to promote moral behavior. If moral behavior increased, we might not have ones like at the Company picnic. The receptionist wrote down our answers.

1. Morality is a constant but can be applied differently by different people.
2. Our moral compass was drifting to far off course.
3. If the Company's moral compass continued to drift off course, its days were numbered.
4. The Company should develop morals and morality committee to promote moral conduct.
5. If moral behavior increased, perhaps incidents like those at the Company picnic wouldn't happen.

We finished up, and I headed to my office to meet with the Consultant. When I arrived, he wasn't there. *Hmm,* I thought. *He had been here the previous two days. Perhaps he'd be along in a moment.* In the meantime, I logged into Facebook to see if anyone had posted anything about the training. I had to laugh. The Consultant had made a post. It said, "Great training today, everyone!" He had tagged everyone in his post, most of them commented back that they were enjoying the training. One comment, though, drew my attention. It was subtle, but it clearly alluded to what the Consultant and I had discussed, the perception of my *alleged* promiscuous behavior many believed led to my selection as CEO. I wonder why this individual didn't bring it up during the training.

My office door opened, and the Consultant entered. He took his customary chair across from my desk; only today, he didn't need his iPad. "So," I began, "you're purposely late, aren't you?" I asked.

"Am I?" he asked sheepishly.

"Obviously, you read the comment on Facebook."

He nodded as he pursed his lips.

"What do you think?" I asked.

"I think you need to handle it. You need to address it."

"On Facebook?" I asked a bit surprised.

"Sure. Why not? It's where young people live today. And older people too, for that matter," he added. "Compose a nonemotional response. Invite anyone who has questions to ask them. Address your qualifications and the board's reason for selecting you. Ignoring the issue is only going to give it credence and perpetuate it."

"Hmm," I said aloud. I wasn't sold on the idea. Airing dirty laundry, real or alleged, wasn't my style. But I supposed he did have a point. "Okay," I said. "I will compose something, review it, and post it. It will make for good conversation tomorrow, right?" I asked with a smile.

He said goodbye, rose, and left. Two more days of training to go.

DAY 4
THE REAL THING

Most people struggle to understand the purpose of their leadership. In order to find their purpose, authentic leaders must first understand themselves and their passions. In turn, their passions show the way to the purpose of their leadership.

—Bill George

What is Authentic Leadership

I arrived at the office a little earlier than usual and decided to check Facebook to see if anyone had responded to my post. I was genuinely surprised at how many people commented. Posts ranged from supportive to indifferent. I got the impression some people viewed my post as an attempt to justify my position. *Oh, well,* I thought. *People are going to believe what they want, regardless of what I say.* I was still happy I had made the post, and most of the comments were positive.

When everyone had been seated in the training room, the Consultant greeted us exuberantly as usual. I wondered where he got the energy. "And how is everyone doing today?" he asked. There were the usual monotone comments that people tend to make precoffee. "Excellent," he continued as he conducted a review of yesterday's topic.

When we had finished discussing the previous day's material, he reviewed the climate assessment survey. There were only two comments, and they were both positive. "Today, we are going to discover who you really are," he said as he displayed a slide.

Everyone looked back and forth at each other in jest.

THE REAL THING
THE CURRENCY OF LEADERSHIP

Day 4

"When it comes to the currency, perhaps nothing has more worth than one's personal brand or authenticity." He began to walk around the room. He continued, "Much has been written about authentic leadership in the past few decades. Its very name alone implies genuineness not common to other forms of leadership. I performed a Google search for the term last night, and it returned nearly three million results. It would seem that there is some interest in the concept and no shortage of information available," he said with a smile. "Interestingly enough," he continued, "the Harvard Business School executive education program boasts a course on the very subject, Authentic Leadership Development (ALD), whose purpose is to enable students to develop themselves as leaders of organizations and to embark on paths of personal leadership development."[137]

"What do you think about that?" he asked. "By a show of hands, how many people believe leaders need to be authentic?" He surveyed the room as he mentally counted the raised hands, which to me appeared to be all of them.

"Interesting," he said as he meandered around the room. "Your response supports the premise that people, who hear the term, believe it's a good thing, even though they may not fully understand it." *Well, he got us on that one,* I thought. I had raised my hand, because it sounded good to me.

He continued as he strode around the room. "Authentic leadership deals primarily with the individual and his or her personal leadership journey. The course at Harvard, which I took several years ago, involves a great deal of introspection, group discussions, similar to ones you've been having all week," he said with a smile, "and analysis of one's leadership journey."

Returning to the podium, he read, "The premise of the ALD is that leaders who know themselves well and consciously develop their leadership abilities throughout their lifetimes will be more effective and successful leaders and will lead more satisfying and fulfilling lives."[138] He looked up. "How does that fit with our discussion of values, ethics, and morality?"

"It means that leaders know their values and act in accordance with them," a man from table compassion said.

"Is that a good thing?" the Consultant asked.

"Sure," he said. "Why wouldn't it be?"

"Suppose the leader's values are out of alignment with the organization as well as those in the organization. Would acting in accordance with one's values be beneficial in that case?" the Consultant probed.

"I suppose not, but what you read suggests that a leader who knows his or her values is more apt to be effective."

"Not everyone has the same values," a young girl from table loyalty said. "Who wants a leader whose value is completely different? Who cares if he or she is authentic? What does that really mean anyway?"

The Consultant smiled as he listened to the discussion.

"I want a leader who is authentic," a woman from table respect said. "I want to know who I'm dealing with."

"So authenticity implies a degree of familiarity?" the Consultant asked.

"Yes, because it makes me feel I genuinely know the person and what he or she stands for. In other words, what you see is what you get—no pretense."

"No pretense?" the Consultant asked. "Is that realistic? Don't we all have pretense to a certain extent?"

"Maybe," she said. "But I think the most authentic leaders have less, which is why they seem more genuine."

"This is very interesting," he said. "When I took the course, Bill George was the senior lecturer. [He] describes the authentic leadership approach through five basic characteristics." He displayed a slide on the screen as he read them and elaborated.

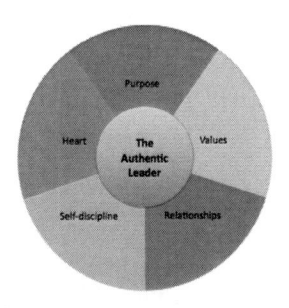

1. "They understand their purpose,
2. They have strong values about the right thing to do,
3. They establish trusting relationships with others,
4. They demonstrate self-discipline and act on their values,
5. They are passionate about their mission i.e. act from their heart."[139]

He paused as he began to walk around the room again. "What are your thoughts about that?" he asked.

"Those qualities sound great," I said. "But they could very easily apply to a bad leader as well as good one. They might be acting on their values, but who's to say those values are good?"

"Excellent point," he said enthusiastically. "Other comments?"

A young lady from table respect said, "I think the idea behind authentic leadership is noble, being a person who has good values and does the right thing. But like she said,"—She gestured at me—"authenticity doesn't necessarily mean it's what you want or that it is good. It's certainly implied."

"I think if we consider the components of authentic leadership as presented, it is a good thing. We can pick apart the definition all day and cite negative examples," said a member of table compassion, "but I don't think that's what this is really all about. It's about being the best person you can be, despite your faults. You learn from them and get better, not worse. And that's what makes a leader authentic."

"Great conversation," the Consultant said. "Let's continue by considering these four key components identified by *Forbes*. I think they will shed some more light on the positive connotations of the term."

He displayed another slide on the screen and asked for a volunteer to read it.

> ### 1. AUTHENTIC LEADERS ARE SELF-AWARE AND GENUINE.
>
> Authentic leaders are self-actualized individuals who are aware of their strengths, their limitations, and their emotions. They also show their real selves to their followers. They do not act one way in private and another in public; they don't hide their mistakes or weaknesses out of fear of looking weak. They also realize that being self-actualized is an endless journey, never complete.

After a member from table loyalty read the slide, the Consultant said, "Thank you. Is there anything that stands out in this slide that we touched on over the past few days?" he asked.

"They act the same all the time, which relates to our discussion on values and having one set of values, one set for work, and one for home," a board member at table compassion said.

"Yes," the Consultant said. "Authentic leaders have one set of values that guides their actions, no matter what the situation is." He advanced the slide and again asked for another volunteer to read it. I jumped on it and read.

> **2. AUTHENTIC LEADERS ARE MISSION DRIVEN AND FOCUSED ON RESULTS.**
>
> They are able to put the mission and the goals of the organization ahead of their own self-interest. They do the job in pursuit of results, not for their own power, money or ego.

"Thank you," he said. "This is a somewhat appropriate slide, given your position with the Company, don't you think?" he asked with a smile. I smiled and nodded. I felt a little awkward at being singled out, given that many CEOs were overpaid and often received lavish compensation packages that incited angst. But I knew the point he was trying to make and let it go.

"How does this relate to values, ethics, and morality?" he asked.

A man from table honesty said, "Well, if you're going to put the organization first, you need values that allow you to do that. You'd have to be ethical and behave morally to really do that."

"What if I was content with my current position and salary and worked hard to serve the needs of others? Would it be possible for me to behave unethically and have questionable moral standards?" he asked. "Does being authentic solve those issues?"

"Authentic leadership doesn't mean you have better values, behave more ethically, or have a sounded character," a woman from table trust said. "Leaders are human. What I think authentic leaders do and bring to the table is experience. They've been through the school of hard knocks. They 'get it,' in a way. Can they make mistakes? Sure. The difference, I think, is they've looked real hard in the mirror and know who they really are. They know their flaws and understand their character. And many of them have made mistakes but they've learned from them."

"Excellent point," the Consultant said. "To summarize, authentic leaders strive to adhere to their values, behave ethically, and establish a genuine moral standard that is reflected in their actions. Does everyone agree?"

Everyone nodded, and a man from table honesty said, "I think a good example of what we're talking about can be found in a recent news story." He looked around the room. "Some of you might recall the story about Raymond Burse, the interim president of Kentucky State University, who announced that he would take a twenty-five-percent salary cut to boost their wages.[140] Some people might think he did it as a publicity stunt, but if so, it's an awfully expensive one."

"I recall that story," the Consultant said. "Very intriguing. Do you believe he took the pay cut out of genuine sincerity and concern for the lower paid workers, or were his actions predicated on feeding his ego, the need for notoriety?"

"I believe it was genuine," I said. "I followed the story in the news, and I saw him interviewed. He appeared very sincere. Although, he took a significant reduction in his salary, he's still earning a decent paycheck." I smiled. I could personally relate to the situation.

> **3. AUTHENTIC LEADERS LEAD WITH THEIR HEART, NOT JUST THEIR MINDS.**
>
> They are not afraid to show their emotions, their vulnerability and to connect with their employees. This does not mean authentic leaders are "soft." In fact communicating in a direct manner is critical to successful outcomes, but it's done with empathy; directness without empathy is cruel.

After a member of table trust read the slide, the Consultant asked, "What do you think this slide is really saying?"

"I think it means they are real people," a woman from table loyalty said.

"Please elaborate," the Consultant said.

"They don't take everything in stride and tow the company line all the time. When something goes wrong, they aren't afraid to show their emotions. They keep it real."

"Ah, I see," the Consultant said. "They don't put on a façade and pretend to act differently for the benefit of others."

> ### 4. AUTHENTIC LEADERS FOCUS ON THE LONG-TERM.
>
> A key tenet in Bill George's model is the company leaders are focused on long-term shareholder value, not in just beating quarterly estimates. Just as George did as CEO of   , and as Bezos has done for years at Amazon, leaders realize that to nurture individuals and to nurture a company requires hard work and patience, but the approach pays large dividends over time.
>
> Kevin Kruse, "What is Authentic Leadership?" Forbes (May 12, 2013)

A member from my table read the slide, and the Consultant asked, "So what does this mean in terms of values and ethics?"

"It means, they value people over profits," a member from table compassion said.

"Spot on," the Consultant said. "You are right on the money."

He wrapped up the conversation as time ran out. It was time for our morning break before heading into our small group. I had to admit, I was really enjoying the group discussion, and I looked forward to the small groups. I was learning about the Company and the importance of quality leadership.

Integrity

Our topic this morning was integrity. It was the facilities manager's second turn leading the group. He thumbed through the folder as he introduced the topic.

"When I was in the Navy, I worked for a Master Chief Petty Officer—Tim Clemmons—I still remember his name, who frequently stated, 'Your integrity must be beyond reproach.' What he meant by that statement is an individual must be absolutely credible. To achieve such credibility, an individual needed to act, not just in accordance with established standards, but one needed to exceed them at all times—both at work and at home. In other words, one's character must remain intact at all times and remain unscathed under extreme scrutiny. He set a high standard, and he established the idea of integrity as the true measure of character and leadership."

"I like that," the account executive said. "That's a great analogy."

I nodded. I thought that was pretty good too.

The facilities manager read from a sheet in the folder. "The word *integrity* is derived from the Latin word *integri*, meaning wholeness. It is defined as a state of being whole or undiminished. It is also defined as a state of soundness of and adherence to moral principle."[141] He looked up and asked us what are thoughts were.

The shipping clerk spoke first. "I think it sounds very similar to what we discussed this morning regarding authentic leadership."

"Integrity is who you *really* are, not simply who you profess to be," added the receptionist. "You can't fake integrity."

I decided to add to the group. "When I think of integrity, I recall the titles from two songs by The Who, 'Can You See the Real Me?' and 'Who Are You?' While the songs don't deal with the issue of integrity, the titles do relate to the topic, because they call into question the underlying element of one's being and its visibility."

"The implication," began the account manager, "is that a person's integrity is not always clearly defined, right?"

"I wouldn't [say] it's not clearly defined," I responded. "The reason I mentioned the song titles is because I don't think we're always aware of who we are. To me, the song titles suggest an introspection of the self. We have to know who we are, which isn't always easy to figure out, because most of us believe we're someone we aren't. Sometimes, it's more obvious to others than it is to ourselves."

He continued, "So you're saying we put on an act for others?"

"Not just others," I said. "We put on the act for ourselves too. It's not easy facing the person staring back in the mirror sometimes." He nodded, accepting my answer in silence.

"What do you mean by that?" asked the facilities manager.

"Well," I said, "have you ever looked in the mirror and asked yourself who you are? Perhaps you found yourself in a situation in which you believed you would act differently but didn't, and now you are questioning your identity as a person."

"I suppose," he said.

The receptionist added, "Deep down, we all have a sense of who we really are, but can others see that? Is it perceptible, or is our integrity something that we are able to control for others to see? Is it ingrained in us and free from alteration?"

"You know," broke in the shipping clerk, "there is line from the movie *Fight Club* that comes to mind when it comes to the subject of integrity. 'Who you were in fight club is not who you were in the rest of the world.' In other words, integrity is a façade—a guise adorned for the others."

"You really believe integrity can be faked?" asked the account manager. "I saw the movie and understand the meaning of the line you quoted."

"I don't know if it can be faked," the shipping clerk responded. "I believe, what the line implies is that the *real you* was saved for later for a select few and lurked beneath the surface—at least, in that particular situation."

"True," I said. "Some view integrity as a controllable element of one's character. That is, what you do when no one is looking as opposed to your observable behavior."

"Yes," the facilities manager said. "It's analogous to the age-old question, 'If a tree falls in a forest and there is no one there to observe it, does it make a sound?' If confronted with a moral challenge and no one is there to observe it, how will someone act?"

The account executive chimed in. "An important consideration about this synopsis is it presupposes how one acts when no one is looking and is demonstrative of one's complete character, and if one experiences a moral failure, it represents one's integrity as a whole. It's true, the whole is the sum of its parts, but we must remember that just because people are fallible, does not mean they are completely bad."

"Yes," the facilities manager said as he prepared to read from a document in the folder. "Colonel Kail, course director of military leadership at the US Military Academy at West Point, observed there are two critical components of integrity that go beyond just doing the right thing when no one is looking. The first is the adherence to a moral or ethical principle. This isn't simple compliance to a rule; it implies a philosophical understanding of the reason it exists. The second is the pursuit of an undiminished state or condition. Everyone makes mistakes, so being a person of integrity does not mean you haven't committed a moral or ethical violation—ever. It means having the strength of character to learn from those *misbehaviors* and seek continual self-improvement."[142]

"Those are great points," said the receptionist. "Integrity is not a one-shot deal. It's developed over time through experience."

"I agree," I said. "Integrity isn't flawless; its value lies not in perfection. Rather, as Colonel Kail noted, its value rests in the pursuit of a higher standard and overcoming moral shortcomings."

The facilities manager nodded, glanced at the sheet, and then asked, "Why is integrity vital to the leader-follower relationship?"

The receptionist said, "Well, speaking for myself and my position in the Company, followers often know little or nothing about a leader." She gave me a furtive glance. "We seek available information to fill the void and develop an opinion or judgment of a leader, based on behavioral observations, for instance, integrity."[143]

The account executive said, "Leader integrity matters, because it plays a significant role in the decision process used by followers when deciding who they will follow, who they will trust, to whom they will be loyal and committed, and ultimately, for whom they will perform."[144]

"It's like we said at the beginning of this discussion, integrity is character currency and individual credibility. Therefore, it's the epicenter of the leader-follower relationship, because it serves as a leader's identity to his or her followers by offering information to support important judgments about [a] leader's likely behavior and their values and ethical orientations."[145]

I added to his comment, "Integrity answers the question I posed earlier in the song title, 'Can you see the real me?' for followers."

"That's right," the shipping clerk said, looking right at me. "And they're looking for the *real* you all the time. Subordinates keep track of seniors' behavior and conduct. They watch everything. Therefore, integrity is always being measured."

"Yes," I said. "I agree. A leader's effectiveness is directly affected by his or her integrity."

We finished our discussion and headed to lunch.

The Genuine Article

After lunch, the Consultant greeted everyone with enthusiasm. "How was your small group discussion?"

The responses rang out.

"Excellent."

"Informative."

"Eye-opening."

"Terrific."

"I am happy to hear that," he said. He spent about five minutes reviewing integrity and our small group discussions. "We are going to elaborate on this morning's discussion and that of your small group discussion. As we consider authentic leadership, we are going to discuss what differentiates authentic leadership from other forms of leadership and why is it so popular." He began to walk around the room.

"In regard to values and the individual," he said, "authentic leaders are who they are all the time. They embody their values in all situations, whether at work or home. Thus," he said with a smile, "they main their integrity in all situations." He paused and stood still. "Do leaders have a separate set of values for work and another for home? What are your thoughts?"

"I don't think it's possible to have more than one set of values, period," a man from table compassion said.

"I agree," a young lady from table respect said. "People might try to have different values at home and work, but I think in the end, what they really value will shine through, regardless of the situation."

"Ah," the Consultant said. "You mean their integrity, or perhaps lack thereof," he smiled, "is a constant that is not subject to change?"

"Well," she responded, "people can act out of character in different situations. We're not robots. If we're tired, hungry, in a mad mood, or whatever, we can deviate from our norm. But when the dust settles, who we are is who we are. We're not going to stray so far as to have different values at home and work."

"I see," he said. "In your survey responses, sixty-six percent of you indicated you did not believe it was possible to have more than one set of values, which indicates that leaders are true to themselves. They don't have a separate set of values for the office and their home life."

"So in consideration of authentic leadership," a member of table honesty said, "values determine who you are, and that is the origin of one's authentic leadership, right?"

The Consultant nodded. "'Leadership has to be coming from who you are. You have to be authentic and be the genuine you. You have to be the real person that you're called to be.'[146] He paused for effect. "In other words, leaders have to be the real thing, the genuine article." He referred us to a page in our student guide, which contained an excerpt from an article.

> In the early 1970s, Coca Cola featured an advertising campaign with a large crowd of people singing: "I'd like to buy the world a Coke and keep it company

> (*refrain:* That's the real thing)." When people hear authentic, they associate it with the real thing, the genuine article, not an imitation or knockoff, i.e., an authentic Ming vase, an authentic Rolex, an authentic Picasso, etc. In other words, the brand remains intact and retains its worth as determined by its intrinsic value, which is what the consumer expects and demands. Leadership is no different. Followers want the real thing![147]

When we had finished reading, the Consultant asked, "Do you agree with the article?"

One of the board members at table trust, who had been fairly silent throughout the training, spoke. "I concur. Leaders cannot simply put on an act or 'staged behavior,'[148] which is all too often the case. Only genuine leadership will suffice."

"Staged behavior?" the Consultant asked. "You mean, it can't be a game face, right?"

The board member simply nodded.

"Excellent!" he said. "That brings us back to our original question regarding authentic leadership. In defining authentic leadership, Michael Hyatt lists five essential elements."

He displayed a slide.

After it was read, he asked, "How would you simplify the information in this slide?"

"I think, it means a leader needs common sense," I said. "Many leaders are insulated from the real issues, and they're told what other think they want to hear. They get caught up in data analysis and numbers. Sometimes, you need to step back and get some perspective. See the big picture." *That's certainly my experience,* I thought.

"Great point," he said. "Other thoughts?"

"I think she's right," a member from my table said. "Too many leaders have no clue what's really going in an organization. They need to walk among their people and know the pulse of the Company."

"Super!" he said as he advanced the slide.

> ### AUTHENTIC LEADERS HAVE *INSIGHT*.
>
> Sometimes we refer to this as *vision*, but that usually has exclusive reference to the future. While leaders must have vision, they need more. They need wisdom and discernment. They need to be able to look at complex situations, gain clarity, and determine a course of action.

> ## AUTHENTIC LEADERS DEMONSTRATE *INITIATIVE.*
>
> They go first. They don't sit on the sidelines. They don't ask others to do what they are unwilling to do themselves. Instead, they lead by example. Lt. Col. Hal Moore is a great example of this. Famously depicted by Mel Gibson in the movie, Lt. Moore told his troops, before leaving for Vietnam. "We are going into battle against a tough and determined enemy. I can't promise you that I will bring you all home alive. But this I swear, before you and before Almighty God: that when we go into battle, I will be the first to set foot on the field, and I'll be the last to step off. And I will leave no one behind. Dead or alive, we will all come home together, so help me God."

"What do you think about this?" he asked.

"That sounds good," a member from table trust said. "But you don't see too many leaders who are willing to do that. Most of them sit back and tell everyone what to do. And they're too far removed from the real issues to fully understand the ramifications of their decisions."

"Why do suppose that is?" he probed.

"Well, probably because, like Cheryl said,"—he motioned at me—"many leaders are insulated from the real issues and are told what others think they want to hear. So they end up making bad decisions."

"Interesting," the Consultant said. "So you believe leaders need to be engaged with their people on a regular basis?"

"Absolutely."

"Okay," he said, "moving on." He displayed the next slide. "Why is influence important?"

> **AUTHENTIC LEADERS EXERT *INFLUENCE*.**
>
> It's no coincidence that *influence* and *influenza* (the flu) come from the same root word. Real leaders are contagious. People "catch" what they have. People are drawn to their vision and their values. They are able to gather a following and move people to act. To change metaphors, they are like *human wave pools,* creating a ripple effect wherever they go.

"Influence is everything," a woman at table loyalty said. "Influence is how leaders get things done."

"And it's also how the train goes off the tracks too," a man from table respect said. "What do you mean by that?" the Consultant asked.

"I mean," the man said, "a leader can influence how others act without knowing it. For example, if a supervisor leaves early because his or her supervisor has already left or is absent and doesn't properly document it, subordinates might be indirectly influenced to act similarly. That's how corner-cutting happens."

"Is that common?" the Consultant asked. *Good question,* I want to know the answer to that too.

"I don't know that it's common," he said, "but it doesn't have to be."

"Why not?" asked the Consultant.

"Because we're talking about influence, and influence only has to be subtle to be effective."

The Consultant pursed his lips and nodded.

> **AUTHENTIC LEADERS HAVE *IMPACT*.**
>
> At the end of the day, leaders make a difference. The world is changed because of their leadership. They are able to create real and lasting change. The measure of leadership cannot be found in the leader; it is found in the impact the leader has on his or her followers.

"So," the Consultant said as he advanced the slide, "because leaders exert influence, they have an impact on the organization, right?"

"Yes," a young lady from table honesty said. "But that doesn't always mean it's a positive impact."

"Very true," the Consultant said, advancing the slide. "You discussed integrity in your small group this morning. Integrity goes hand in hand with authentic leadership, don't you agree?"

> ### AUTHENTIC LEADERS EXERCISE *INTEGRITY.*
>
> Not every leader is benevolent. Adolf Hitler was a leader, as was Mao Zedong and Josef Stalin. They had insight, initiative, influence, and impact. Yet their lives were not *integrated* with the highest values. Integrity—or the lack thereof—ultimately determines the quality of a person's impact. In a sense, this is the foundation of authentic leadership.
>
> Michael Hyatt, "The Five Marks of Authentic Leadership," *MichaelHyatt.com*.

"I agree," I said. "Based on everything we've discussed thus far, I believe authentic leaders are those individuals who remain true to themselves, regardless of circumstances. They maintain their values. An authentic leader has an ethical core. She or he knows the right thing to do and is driven by a concern for ethics and fairness.[149] Authentic leadership is integrally linked to one's values and ethical behavior."

"Fantastic!" he said. "You are right on target. In order to be a truly authentic leader, though, one must do more than simply identify his or her values. An authentic leader is one who knows his or her values because they have been tested."

He returned to the podium and read a quote, "The values that form the basis for authentic leadership are derived from your beliefs and convictions, but you will not know what your true values are until they are tested under pressure. Having a solid base of values and testing them under fire enables you to develop the principles you will use in leading."[150]

"That is true," a member from table respect said. "Indeed, one cannot know oneself until his or her mettle has been tested, and one cannot be an authentic leader, as outlined in the principles discussed, unless his or her values are in alignment with subordinates, peers, seniors, and the organization. Aligning one's values with these elements requires congruity that cannot be faked."

"Agreed," the Consultant said. "Other thoughts?"

"Authenticity demands that genuineness of character [be] align with established values," a young man from table honesty said.

"Yes," the Consultant said. "A leader's *brand* must be genuine. It must be the *real thing*, based on values, in order to be authentic. Let me conclude by reading you an excerpt.

> Nevertheless, values play a pivotal role in authenticity. They provide a point from which a leader can begin to maneuver; however, standing alone they are not singularly authenticity's composite. Authenticity is a

process by which a leader develops values conducive to the organization in relation to self. Authenticity is more than an individual's connection to self. It is the ever-evolving process of discovery rooted in the self but existent within the confines of relationships amid congruent values. Leadership involves personal branding which plays a pivotal role in creating value. [Authenticity] emerges from the discovery and realization of what is true to one's nature. It then becomes an individual's brand and defines the perception others will formulate in regard to it. Additionally, it will create brand value. However, the brand—the authentic self—must be comprised of the requisite attributes deemed essential by those who give it value. After all, a brand only has as much value as others ascribe to it. And a leader is only as authentic as others believe him or her to be. Therefore, authenticity is a branding process based on the evolution and discovery of individual identity that involves morals, ethics, values, and behavior as it relates to others and the organization."[151]

Very intriguing, I thought.

He looked up from the podium and surveyed the room. "Authenticity, particularly as it relates to leadership, involves being to true to one's values and character, which are developed over the course of time. Being an authentic leader is a matter of developing the authentic self that is congruent and compatible with others and the organization. At the very center of authenticity lies a core that is comprised of desired values and morality that is the composite of one's credibility and integrity. What you are going to discuss in your small group is the effect narcissism can have on leadership and integrity."

That should be interesting, I thought.

Narcissism

It was the receptionist's second time leading the group. When she entered the conference room, she admitted this was going to be interesting topic. "I can't imagine how narcissism has anything to do with values and leadership," she said.

Once she got settled, she quickly thumbed through the folder and scanned the documents. "Okay," she began. "Narcissism, as some of you may know, is based on the Greek myth of Narcissus, a youth who fell in love with his own reflection in the waters of a spring and pined away."

She handed each of us a sheet and said, "We are going to take a quiz to see how where we stand in regard to narcissism."

Sign #1: Unilateral listening.

What I want and what I have to say are all that matters when we talk together. When we make decisions, what you want, your concerns, your feelings…these are mere whispers, inconveniences and irrelevancies. When we discuss issues, my opinions are right. Yours are wrong or else of minimal importance. If you expect to have input, you are undermining me.

Narcissistic listening focuses on how to dismiss, negate, ignore, minimize, denigrate or otherwise render irrelevant other people's concerns.

One sign of narcissistic non-listening: a tone of contempt instead of interest. Another: frequent responses that begin with "*But…,*" which is linguistically a backspace-delete key.

Score: 0 1 2 3 4 5 6 7 8 9 10
Sign #2: It's all about me.

I know more, I know better, I'm more interesting, when we talk, it's mostly about me. In conversations, I take up most of the airtime. Almost all of my chatter is about what I have done, what I am thinking about.

If you begin to talk about yourself, I link back to something in my life so that the focus of the discussion again turns onto me. Maybe that's why people say I suck up all the air in a room.

When I want something, I need to have it. Never mind how you feel about it; it's all about me. I'm big and important and you are merely also here, mostly to do things for me, like a third arm.

Score: 0 1 2 3 4 5 6 7 8 9 10
Sign #3: The rules don't apply to me.

I can have affairs, cut into a line where others are waiting, cheat on my taxes, and ignore rules that get in the way of my doing what I want. Rules are for other people to follow.

Narcissists suffer from what I call Tall Man Syndrome. They experience themselves as above others, so the rules don't apply to them.

Score: 0 1 2 3 4 5 6 7 8 9 10
Sign #4: Your concerns are really criticisms of me, and I hate being criticized.

If you insist on my listening and taking your concerns seriously I'm likely to get mad. Criticism hurts. I can criticize others, and often do, but if you criticize me you're hurting my feelings so I'll hurt you back. And if you say you are at all unhappy, that's a way of indirectly criticizing me. Since "it's all about me" your feelings must be about what I have been doing.

Narcissists paradoxically manifest both an inflated idea of their own importance and quickness to feel deflated by negative feedback.

In addition, because they think everything is about them, they hear others' attempts to talk about personal feelings as veiled criticisms of themselves.

The clinical term for taking others' concerns as personal criticism is *personalizing*, e.g., if she says "I'm feeling lonely," her narcissistic friend will hear the self-statement as an accusation, "You don't spend enough time with me."

Score: 0 1 2 3 4 5 6 7 8 9 10
Sign #5: When things go wrong between us, it's always your fault.

I can't be expected to apologize or to admit blame. I'm above others and above reproach. You shouldn't have... Don't threaten me with expecting me to say how I've contributed to a problem or I'll get mad at you.

Unwillingness to take responsibility for mistakes goes hand in hand with quickness to blame. This trait may come from confusing the part with the whole. "If I've done one thing that's not right, then I must be all bad." That's also all-or-nothing thinking.

Whatever the source of the sensitivity to criticism and difficulty admitting mistakes, the upshot is a tendency to blame others when anything has gone wrong. Blaming and fault-finding in others feel safer to narcissists than looking to discover, learn and grow from their own part in difficulties.

While narcissists are quick to blame, they may be slow to appreciate. Appreciation and gratitude require listening.

Score: 0 1 2 3 4 5 6 7 8 9 10
Sign #6: If I'm angry, it's your fault.

You made me mad. You didn't listen to me. You criticized me. You're trying to control me. Your view is wrong. So you need to apologize, not me.

I'm not responsible either for my anger. If I'm mad, it's because I'm frustrated by what you are doing. My anger is your fault. I'm only made because you ... "

Some narcissists show major charm and social agility. At the same time, these seemingly super-confident folks also can be quick to anger. When they do become inflamed, they then immediately blame their anger on others.

What are typical anger triggers for people with narcissistic tendencies?

Critical comments will do it. As I said above, as much as narcissisitc folks see themselves as special, they also can be remarkably thin-skinned. Any feedback that punctures their belief in total specialness can feel quite threatening. The immediate response will be to issue blame.

Telling anyone what to do, or sounding even somewhat like you are telling them what to do, also is likely to provoke irritation. Pretty much everyone prefers autonomy (unless the two people have an agreed-upon boss-worker or similar relationship). Narcissists however tend to be hyper-sensitive about feeling controlled. Any request therefore to a narcissist is at risk for sounding to them like a demand and therefore triggering irritation.

Asking someone who is narcissistic to do something your way rather than theirs is particularly likely to sound to them like you are telling them what to do. Their anger in response, of course, is *your* fault.

Score: 0 1 2 3 4 5 6 7 8 9 10
Total Score: ___ What does this score indicate?

The interpretations below are based on my clinical hunches, not any scientific testing. They're meant just to give you a general indicate of what your quiz suggests.

Scores that total 5–10 probably indicate normal human fallibilities with room for improvement. No one is perfect. If you think you are perfect, and scored therefore below 5, you might check again. Be sure your scores do not indicate a narcissism of excessive belief that you are perfect, another potential sign of narcissism

Too much narcissism in your habits would be indicated by a total score of 10 to 30. Pay attention to your "narcissism lite" and you may fairly easily be able to lower that score considerably.

A total score of 30 or higher spells significant narcissistic habits that probably do not serve you well. Time to make some serious habit changes!

40 to 60 would indicate to me severe problems with narcissism. With this understanding of why your relationships become distressed, hopefully you will commit yourself to some serious personal growth.[152]

After we finished scoring our quizzes, the Receptionist said, "Okay, how did everyone do?"

We laughed. Apparently, we were all a bit narcissistic.

"So what does narcissism have to do with leadership?" asked the facilities manager.

The Receptionist read from a sheet in the folder. "It says here that a moderate amount of narcissism may be a positive trait."[153]

"How can that be?" the account executive asked.

"Well," the Receptionist began as she read from the document, "Narcissists tend to be extraverted, and that [leads] to the positive relationship between narcissism and leader emergence.[154] Also, leaders, such as Jack Welch and George Soros, are examples of productive narcissists. They are gifted and creative strategists who see the big picture and find meaning in the risky challenge of changing the world and leaving behind a legacy. Indeed, one reason we look to productive narcissists in times of great transition is that they have the audacity to push through the massive transformations that society periodically undertakes. Productive narcissists are not only risk-takers willing to get the job done but also charmers who can convert the masses with their rhetoric."[155]

The account executive laughed a little. "What you're saying reminds me of functional autism in a way. It's as though narcissist have a handicap that, for the most part, impedes productivity. Yet there are exceptions [of narcissists] who are productive."

"Yeah," the facilities manager added. "But is narcissism a good thing or not?"

"I think too much of any personality trait is not good," I said. "Over the years, I've taken a number of personality tests, or more frequently known as temperament sorters, and I can tell you people are not that simple. You can't pigeonhole someone into a single category and slap a label on someone."

The receptionist spoke as she read from the folder, "A new study published this month in the journal *Personnel Psychology* tried to answer that question, doing what academics call a 'meta-analysis' of existing research on narcissism and organizational performance. What they found was that narcissists are more likely to reach leadership positions, but there was no consensus answer for how much narcissism really affects a leader's success. Disappointed they had nothing to show for [in] their analysis, the researchers decided to use data from HR consulting firm, Hogan Assessment Systems, to try to find out whether a happy medium exists instead. 'I was surprised no one had ever checked,' said Peter Harms, a management professor at the University of Nebraska at Lincoln and one of the study's co-authors. 'There must be somewhere between a total lack of confidence and malignant self-esteem,' he said, that would be appropriate for good leadership.

"As it turned out, they were right. By analyzing personality assessments and performance evaluations from six data sets, the researchers found that the relationship between narcissism and leadership effectiveness took on the shape of an upside-down *U*. The leadership ratings of those at the extremes (the insecure and the timid on one side, and the toxic self-aggrandizers on the other) were poor, while those in the middle did very well. 'The ancient Greeks were right,' Harms said. Everything in moderation. Harms says that if companies choose to screen for narcissism in their hiring practices or personality assessments of leaders,— say, not hiring or promoting anyone who rates in the top or bottom ten percent—they should first do an internal evaluation of what an optimal level is for their organization. What rates as average levels of ego and confidence at a hospital, for instance, might be very different than at a Wall Street bank.

"And then, of course, narcissism has to be taken in context. 'A narcissist who's not very smart or hard-working is a disaster,' Harms said. 'But a narcissist who's really smart and really hardworking could end up being someone brilliant, like Steve Jobs.'[156]"

"So how do we measure the right amount of narcissism at the Company?" the shipping clerk asked.

Good question, I thought. "I can answer that," I said. "We don't really. We have an interview process that is handled by HR. They assess certain personality attributes based on the position, but there are no specific questions for identifying narcissism."

"Oh, okay," he said.

I continued. "Most of the positions within the Company don't require screening for narcissism. Furthermore, as I stated earlier, even if we had a test to identify narcissistic characteristics, no one can be classified that simply. Human beings are much more complex than that." I realized I was monopolizing the conversation and glanced at everyone as a means of inviting others to add to the conversation.

The account executive picked up on my gesture and said, "I agree. I took several psychology classes in college—I wanted to be psychologist, or so I thought—and I recall Freud divided personalities into three types: erotic, obsessive, and narcissistic. Most of us have elements of all three."[157]

"Why is that?" asked the shipping clerk.

"We are all, for example, somewhat narcissistic. If that were not so, we would not be able to survive or assert our needs. The point is, one of the dynamic tendencies usually dominates the others, making each of us react differently to success and failure."[158]

"That makes sense," he said. "I get that. I don't think many people are truly narcissistic. Like you said,"—he gestured at me—"you can't pigeonhole someone's personality that easily."

"So how does narcissism relate to values and ethics?" the facilities manger asked, directing his question to group leader.

The receptionist looked down at the folder and read, "Narcissism is a human personality trait that shows promise in partially explaining individuals' departure from solid ethical judgment. Narcissists tend to ignore the rules that govern the behavior of others, to attain personal goals at the expense of others, and to be insensitive to what society expects of them in terms of conformity to its norms. Therefore, a person might be seduced by his or her own narcissism into engaging in acts that are unethical and possibly illegal."[159]

Interesting, I thought. "It seems preoccupation with oneself can lead to egregious errors in judgment, which is not a good leadership trait," I said.

"That seems logical," the account executive said. "If an individual is too preoccupied with himself or herself and [personal] interests, the line between right and wrong could easily become blurred."

"Do you think that's what happened with the Company?" the Receptionist asked flatly.

"What do you mean?" the facilities manager asked.

"What I mean is the breaches in ethics that were brought up in class this week. Do you think they were caused by narcissism?" she asked.

We all sat silently for a moment.

Finally, feeling somewhat obligated, I spoke. "Well, I think it's more complicated than simply labeling it as narcissism. That might be a part of it in some cases, but

I think what led to some of the issues mentioned in class is a lack of oversight and a pattern of behavior that was never addressed. Therefore, it was accepted as the norm. Were some of the people involved narcissistic? Probably, but there's no way to say it with any certainty."

"I think the lesson here," the shipping clerk added, "is everyone needs to be aware of his or her motives and not be too preoccupied with himself or herself."

We all nodded in agreement as we wrapped up and prepared to head into our last group discussion of the day.

Groupthink

The Consultant greeted us enthusiastically as we entered the training room. "Is anyone feeling narcissistic?" he asked with a smile.

We all laughed as we took our seats.

"It must have seemed strange to study narcissism in light of the overall topic, but I trust you each have a keen understanding of how it relates to ethics, values, and behavior." He surveyed the room as many heads nodded. "Good," he said and conducted a brief review of the topic.

When he finished, he said, "Just as narcissism relates to the individual, groupthink can also have a tremendous impact on behavior."

He stood at the podium and displayed a slide.

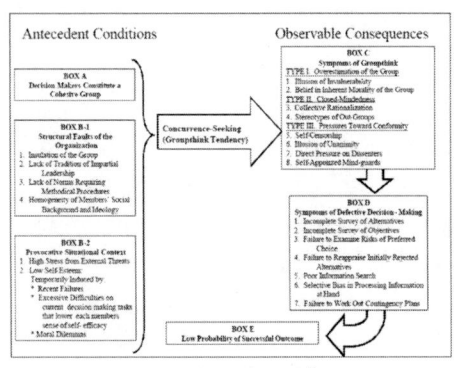

Figure 1. The Groupthink Model[12]

He read from a document. "Groupthink is a term first used in 1972 by social psychologist, Irving L. Janis, that refers to a psychological phenomenon in which people strive for consensus within a group. In many cases, people will set aside their own personal beliefs or adopt the opinion of the rest of the group. People, who are opposed to the decisions or overriding opinion of the group as a whole, frequently remain quiet, preferring to keep the peace rather than disrupt the uniformity of the crowd."[160]

After reading, he began to walk around the room. "What do you think?" he asked. "Is this true?"

"It must be true," a member from table compassion said, "because you read it. Now, if you mean is it true here, I don't know. I can't recall a time when I was involved with a group where people didn't speak their minds."

The Consultant smiled. "Well, I'm glad to here that. However, do you think this happens here?"

I jumped on that one. "Absolutely," I said. "I've been to many meetings where people remained silent about what they thought, although I could read their facial expressions. They would come up to me, or someone who'd been at the meeting, and voice their opinion after everyone left."

"And why do you think they did that?" he asked.

"Because they didn't want to rock the boat or displease a superior," I said.

"Exactly!" he said. "And as a result, groupthink occurred whether anyone knew it or not."

He returned to the podium and read from another document, "[Groupthink] is excessive to the extent that the group members have come to value the group (and their being part of it) higher than anything else. This causes them to strive for a quick and painless unanimity on the issues that the group has to confront. To preserve the clubby atmosphere, group members suppress personal doubts, silence dissenters, and follow the group leader's suggestion. They have a strong belief in the inherent *morality* [emphasis mine] of the group, combined with a decidedly evil picture of the group's opponents. The results are devastating: a distorted view of reality, excessive optimism producing hasty and reckless policies, and a neglect of *ethical issues* [emphasis mine]."[161]

Everyone murmured. The Consultant stood silently and let his words sink in. "So," he said at last, "let us consider groupthink in light of narcissism. How do the two relate?"

"If you have a narcissist who is part of a group, it could lead to unethical behavior, especially since members of the group value being part of it so highly," a member from table compassion said.

"Yes," the Consultant said. "What else?"

A young woman from table respect said, "Narcissists tend to deviate from established moral and ethical standards. If you have a narcissist in a group or a group of narcissists who believe they are morally superior…well, it would be pretty easy to go down the wrong road and fully believe in what you are doing."

"It sure would," he said. "When it comes to groupthink though, does it necessarily mean unethical behavior will occur?"

"No," a board member from table respect said. I could tell he was taking some of this personally. "Just because a group of people are insulated from others in an organization doesn't mean they intend to do anything unethical."

The Consultant was quick to jump on that. "Ah, you said *intend*. Can groupthink be a precursor to unethical behavior, whether intended or not?" he asked.

"I suppose," the board member said. "But just because groupthink occurs doesn't mean there's anything unethical happening."

"You're right," The Consultant said, moving quickly back to the podium. He read, "The organizational culture may promote the assumption of responsibility for actions taken by individuals and groups thereby increasing the probability that both will behave in an ethical manner. Alternatively, the culture may diffuse responsibility for the consequences of unethical behavior, thereby making such behavior more likely. In addition, there is the increased potential for groupthink, a precursor to organizational counternorms [sic] and unethical behavior."[162]

"So the culture is a key component to groupthink?" asked a member of table loyalty.

"Yes," the Consultant said. "Let's take a look at some organizational symptoms that stem directly from its culture that can lead to groupthink." He displayed a slide and asked for a volunteer to read it. After which, he elaborated on the bullets. "They say there is safety in numbers. Do you believe that holds true for those experience groupthink?"

"Yes," a man from table honesty answered. "I was in a fraternity in college, and I believed I was always protected when I was with my frat brothers."

"Great analogy," the Consultant said. "What about rationalizing a collective effort?"

"Earlier, we discussed narcissists and how strong-willed they are," a woman from table compassion said. "If you had one in a group, or more for that matter, who believed in a particular course of action, they'd easily be able to persuade others to go along."

> ## SYMPTOMS
>
> - An illusion of invulnerability shared by most or all members of the group.
> - Collective efforts to rationalize the group's course of action.
> - Unquestioned belief in the group's inherent morality.
> - Stereotyped views of those not in the group.
> - Direct pressure on any member who expresses strong arguments against any of the group's stereotypes.
> - The emergence of self-appointed mindguards
>
> Ronald Sims, *Ethics and Organizational Decision Making: A Call for Renewal* (1994), 70, Google Books.

"Exactly," the Consultant said. "We already touched on inherent morality. What about stereotyped views of those not in the group?"

"There's the *haves* and *have-nots*," an older gentleman at table trust said. "Those who have look down on those who don't."

"Hmm," the Consultant said. "Us versus them, right?"

The gentleman nodded. "Yup."

"What about expressing arguments against the group?"

"That's a no-no," a woman from table integrity said with a smile. "You don't go against the group."

"And why not?" he asked.

"Because if you do, you won't be part of the group for very long."

"Indeed," he said exuberantly. "And what about *mindguards*? What is that all about?"

"That's how you keep others in check," I said. "They're the gatekeepers who guard the information that enters the group."

"So they provide a layer of insulation and protect the group, right?" he asked.

"Yes," I said. "They tell group members what they think they want to hear and filter out anything that might be perceived to be contrary to their agenda."

He smiled. "The voice of experience?" he asked playfully. I merely returned his smile. No need to go into detail here.

"Well, then, let's conclude with this: Specifically, the ultimate result of groupthink is that group members become isolated from the world around them. They read positive signs as a reaffirmation of their goals and intentions; they read negative signs as an indication that there are individuals who do not understand what they are doing, and that these individuals should be ignored (and perhaps even punished.) During this entire process, it is common to find the group changing to a belief that its ideals are humanitarian and based on high-minded principles. As a result, no attempt is made by the members to challenge or question the ethics of the group's behavior. A second common observation is high esprit de corps and amiability among the members. This often leads them to believe that those who question their approach or intentions are acting irrationally. Quite often, groupthink is only recognized after a group has made a disastrous decision. When this occurs, the members are apt to ask, 'How could we have been so blind? Why didn't anyone call attention to our errors?' Unfortunately, at the time the group was making its decision(s), it is unlikely that any criticism or questioning of its actions would have been given serious consideration. The following prescriptions are given to reduce the probability of groupthink."[163]

He displayed a slide. This time, rather than asking for a volunteer to read the slides, we read to ourselves in silence. When it was obvious we had finished reading, he commented before advancing through the remaining slides, which we read to ourselves.

LEADER PRESCRIPTIONS

1. Assign everyone the role of critical evaluation.
2. Be impartial, do not state preferences.
3. Assign the devil's advocate role to at least one group member.
4. Use outside experts to challenge the group.

"You can't live in a bubble," he said. "Leaders need honest, accurate feedback. Sometimes people need to hear things they don't want to hear. And there are times when leaders need to bring in outsiders who don't share the organizations opinions and are somewhat neutral." He smiled.

"Organizational leaders need to ensure the culture matches the values. They can do this through training and utilizing focus groups, comprised of individuals from different departments. Diversity is key to providing a broad range of ideas and mechanisms to address issues."

> INDIVIDUAL PRESCRIPTIONS
>
> 1. Be a critical thinker.
> 2. Discuss the group's deliberations with a trusted outsider and report back to the group.

"As I mentioned on day one, critical thinking is imperative. Asking questions and validating the answers is a key component of critical thinking, which is what we have done here this week." He smiled. "Also, take ideas and issues outside of the Company. Solicit input from those who have no stake in it. You might be surprised at what you learn."

> ## PROCESS PRESCRIPTIONS
>
> 1. Periodically break the group into subgroups to discuss the issues.
> 2. Take time to study external factors.
> 3. Hold second-chance meetings to rethink issues before making a commitment.
> 4. Periodically rotate new members into groups and old members out.
>
> Sims, Ronald R. 1992. "Linking Groupthink to Unethical Behavior in Organizations." Journal Of Business Ethics 11, no. 9: 660-661.

"Break the issues down. Get different opinions by bringing new people. Don't rush into something. Sleep on it. And just like a doctor, get a second and third opinion before you commit."

When we had finished reading the slides and making comments, we wrapped up our discussion and separated into groups to prepare our leadership applications. The Consultant reminded us that we would be presenting our recommendations the next day that were based on the critical thinking questions we answered at the end of each day.

He displayed the slide and departed.

Leadership Application

> ### LEADERSHIP APPLICATION
>
> - What is the issue?
> - What are the implications for The Company?
> - Why does it matter?
> - How can The Company promote authentic leadership, integrity and reduce narcissism and groupthink?
> - If authentic leadership and integrity increase, what would be the result?

We had the leadership application down now; so it didn't take us long to answer the questions, which the receptionist again recorded for us.

1. The issue is determining if our leaders are indeed authentic or narcissistic.
2. The implication is that narcissistic leaders may appear genuine, but they may be too preoccupied with their own agendas.

3. A company with its head down or blinders on isn't going to remain relevant very long.
4. The Company can promote adherence to its core values and conduct training to determine if a leader is narcissistic. Reducing groupthink can be accomplished by fostering an open environment and soliciting feedback and criticism.
5. An increase in authentic leader would create more genuine relationships and a better work environment.

I headed to my office, where the Consultant was waiting for me. "Hello," I said. He greeted me back as I sat down opposite him behind my desk.

"How do you think it's going?" he asked.

"I think it's going very well. It seems that everyone is genuinely engaged and learning in the process."

He nodded. "I agree." He remained silent.

"And?" I asked.

"And I think you have your work cut out for you, Cheryl. There have been many lively discussions, both in the full group and small groups. You are definitely heading in the right direction, but you have to keep this momentum going. This isn't a quick-fix by any stretch of the imagination."

"I know," I said. "But this is a good start, and I am very happy with the progress thus far."

"I look forward tomorrow and the group presentations," he said as he rose. "See you then."

He left, and I decided to login into Facebook and see what the comments were today. There were a lot of comments about authentic leadership. Many people didn't believe there were any authentic leaders at the Company. I thought that was a little disturbing, and I didn't particularly like having that on the Company's Facebook page. Then I remembered what we had discussed when it came to groupthink and inviting outside opinions.

Well, this was certainly one way to do that, I thought. Rather than respond to the criticism, I decided to go in a different direction. I began to type. "I think it would be a fun idea to post everyone's narcissism quiz scores—anonymously, of course—on Facebook, and see just how many narcissists we actually have. I think we're all a little narcissistic." *Let's see what they say about that,* I mused to myself.

DAY 5
THE POWER OF LEADERSHIP

The greater the power, the more dangerous the abuse.
—Edmund Burke

Defining Leadership

It was hard to believe today was our last day of training. I had genuinely enjoyed the training, particularly in getting to know many of the employees on a personal level. The small groups were my favorite part of the training. I had really learned a lot.

The Consultant greeted everyone with enthusiasm. "Good morning, everyone!" We greeted him back. He smiled. "Today is our last day of training, and we are going to bring everything we've discussed throughout the week together. We will conclude the training with your small group presentations and training assessments. Does anyone have any questions before we begin?" he asked.

No one did. He spent several minutes reviewing yesterday's topics and the class climate assessments. When he finished, he displayed a slide.

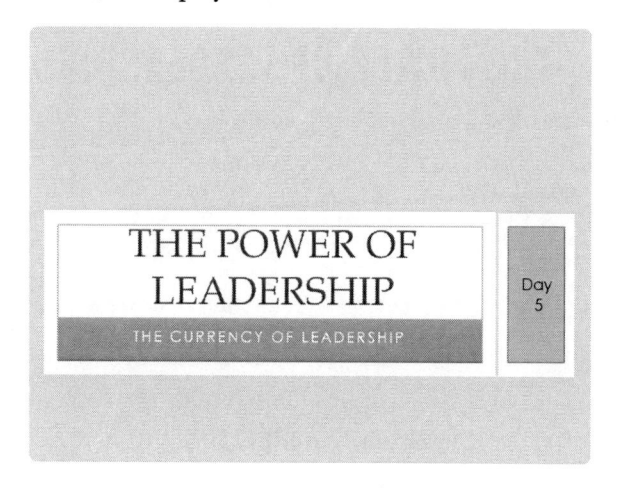

> **THE POWER OF LEADERSHIP**
> THE CURRENCY OF LEADERSHIP
>
> Day 5

"Today," he began as he walked around the room, "we are going to discuss leadership. We are going to look at some definitions of leadership and leadership styles as well as identify some leadership characteristics that give it worth and value." He again alluded to the concept of currency. So," he said, moving to a blank chart, "let's start with table respect. Everyone, please list a characteristic you want to see in a leader."

He then listed all the characteristics on the paper. When we had gone around the room, he stood back and reflected on the list.

honest	integrity	motivated	organized	caring
good listener	empathetic	patient	decisive	influential
proficient	trustworthy	punctual	sympathetic	good communicator
inspiring	supportive	encouraging	ethical	knowledgeable
approachable	genuine	connected	assertive	enthusiastic

"Impressive," he said. "That's quite a list. Let's keep that in mind as we proceed to discuss and define leadership." He moved around the room. "What is leadership?" he asked.

A board member at table honesty said, "According to what I read in John Maxwell's book, leadership is influence—nothing more, nothing less."[164]

"Excellent," he said. That corresponds to the characteristic on our list." He motioned to the chart. "Other definitions and thoughts?"

"Leadership is getting people to do something they don't want to do by creating a desire to do it," a man from table respect said.

"Leadership is an art," a woman from table compassion said.

"An art?" he asked. "What do you mean by that?"

"I mean, you really can't teach it. It takes time and experience to develop. It requires finesse."

"I see," he said. "So leadership training has no benefit?" he asked.

"I'm not saying that. What I mean is you can't give someone a week or two of training and transform him or her into an instant leader. The training might be part of that person's development, but it's not going to happen overnight."

"Agreed," he said. "Let's take a look at some definitions," he said as he displayed a slide.

> ## LEADERSHIP DEFINITIONS
>
> "The only definition of a leader is someone who has followers." – *Peter Drucker*
>
> "Leadership is the capacity to translate vision into reality." – *Warren Bennis*
>
> "If your actions inspire others to dream more, learn more, do more and become more, you are a leader." –*John Quincy Adams*
>
> Read more at http://www.brainyquote.com/quotes/quotes/j/johnquincy386752.html#uAcxOPzuJjQz2gLX.99

"What are you thoughts about these quotes?" he asked after we had read them to ourselves.

"Well, if you're going to be a leader, you're going to need followers," a member from table respect said. "If you don't have followers, you really can't be a leader, can you?"

"I agree," the Consultant said.

A member from table loyalty added, "Leaders definitely need vision."

"Yeah," a man from table trust said. "Leaders should inspire other to excel, and vision is part of that."

"And let's also consider these," the Consultant said as he displayed another slide.

> ## LEADERSHIP DEFINITIONS
>
> "Leadership is the art of getting someone else to do something you want done because he wants to do it." – *Dwight D. Eisenhower*
>
> "Leadership is a privilege to better the lives of others. It is not an opportunity to satisfy personal greed." – *Mwai Kibaki*
>
> "Actions, not words, are the ultimate results of leadership." – *Bill Owens*
>
> Read more at http://www.brainyquote.com/quotes/quotes/b/billowens167728.html#8x3dYDzUHLTTbeFD.99

"Is leadership an art?" the Consultant asked in reference to the first quote.

"Art, skill, talent…take your choice," a board member at table trust said. "Leadership is many things to many people."

"Very true," the Consultant responded.

"Plus," a man from my table added, "not everyone sees a leader the same way. Some people think a leader is the greatest person in the world, while others can't stand him or her."

The Consultant crossed his arms and placed his right hand on his chin and nodded. "Why do you think leadership is so difficult to define?" he asked.

"Because it's subjective," I said. "There is an interpretive quality to leadership based on the expectations and needs of the followers."

"Very impressive," the Consultant said as he made his way back to the podium. "Let me read something to you," he said, reviewing a document.

"A leader is one or more people who selects, equips, trains, and influences one or more follower(s) who have diverse gifts, abilities, and skills and focuses the follower(s) to the organization's mission and objectives, causing the follower(s) to willingly and enthusiastically expend spiritual, emotional, and physical energy in a coordinated effort to achieve the organizational mission and objectives. The leader achieves this influence by humbly conveying a prophetic vision of the future in clear terms that resonates with the follower(s) beliefs and values in such a way that the follower(s) can understand and interpret the future into present-time action steps. In this process, the leader presents the prophetic vision in contrast to the present status of the organization and through the use of critical thinking skills, insight, intuition, and the use of both persuasive rhetoric and interpersonal communication, including both active listening and positive discourse, facilitates and draws forth the opinions and beliefs of the followers such that the followers move through ambiguity toward clarity of understanding and shared insight that results in influencing the follower(s) to see and accept the future state of the organization as a desirable condition worth committing personal and corporate resources toward its achievement. The leader achieves this using *ethical* [emphasis mine] means and seeks the greater good of the follower(s) in the process of action steps such that the follower(s) is/are better off (including the personal development of the follower as well as emotional and physical healing of the follower) as a result of the interaction with the leader. The leader achieves this same state for his/her own self as a leader, as he/she seeks personal growth, renewal, regeneration, and increased stamina–mental, physical, emotional, and spiritual through the leader-follower interactions."[165]

He glanced up, placed the document on the podium, and began to walk around the room. "That's quite a definition, don't you think?" Everyone nodded. "Do you believe it's accurate?"

"Yes," I said. "Leadership is complicated. It can't be pigeonholed into a simple one-line definition."

"Yeah, it's very complex," a woman from table trust said. "I suppose that's why there are so many books on it." She smiled.

"Perhaps," the Consultant retuned her smile. "I think what you're alluding to is that leadership is a process that involves influence, occurs in a group context, and involves goal attainment."[166] He returned to the podium and displayed a slide. "Let's examine the various elements of this definition."

> **PROCESS**
>
> Process implies that a leader affects and is affected by followers. ...it is an interactive event.
>
> Peter Northouse, Leadership, Theory and Practice (California: Sage Publications, 2007), 3.

"What are your thoughts about this?" he asked.

"I agree," a young man from table respect said. "It takes two to tango, as they say, and the same applies to leadership."

"Very good," the Consultant said.

"Leaders also learn from their followers," I said. "I've learned a lot this week, and I can you that leadership is definitely an interactive process that goes both ways."

"Excellent observation," he said.

> ## INFLUENCE
>
> Influence is concerned with how the leader affects followers. Influence is the sine qua non of leadership. Without influence, leadership does not exist.
>
> Peter Northouse, Leadership: Theory and Practice (California: Sage Publications, 2007), 3.

"What exactly is influence?" the Consultant asked.

"It's the ability to change people's thinking and behavior," a man from table honesty said.

"So it's persuasive?" the Consultant prodded.

"It can be," he continued, "but it can also be indirect. What I mean is, a leader can influence a follower's behavior through his example. It can be unintentional and happen without direct effort."

"Similar to the effects of advertising?" the Consultant asked.

"Yes."

"I see."

> **GROUPS**
>
> Groups are the context in which leadership takes place. Leadership involves influencing a group of individuals who have a common purpose.
>
> Peter Northouse, Leadership: Theory and Practice (California: Sage Publications, 2007), 3.

"Why groups?" the Consultant asked.

"Leadership doesn't happen in a vacuum," a man from table compassion said. "It's a collective process."

"A collective process. I like that," the Consultant said. "Indeed, leadership is really a team effort."

> **GOALS**
>
> Leadership includes attention to goals. This means leadership has to do with directing a group of individuals toward accomplishing some task or end.
>
> Peter Northouse, Leadership: Theory and Practice (California: Sage Publications, 2007), 3.

"What purpose do goals serve in leadership?" the Consultant asked.

"They provide a common point of focus," I said, "and serve as a way to unify a group of people."

"Why is unity important?" he asked.

I thought about his question for a few seconds. "Unity provides order and direction. If the group is going in different directions, it will be difficult for the leader to be out in front of everyone, leading in many different directions."

"I see," he said. "Goals provide focus and unite a group." He returned to the podium. "Please keep this conversation in mind when you are in your small groups. I think you will find it enlightening."

Once again, the small group leaders remained behind while the rest of us grabbed coffee and doughnuts and headed to the conference room.

Power and Authority

It was the account executive's second turn to lead the small group. He sat at the table and began by saying, "Power tends to corrupt and absolute power corrupts absolutely."[167] He smiled and continued, "Okay, for this morning's discussion, we are going to discuss the role of power and authority in leadership, particularly how they affect values and ethics."

"This should be fun," the facilities manager said humorously. We all laughed.

"Okay," the account executive said reading from the folder, "The concept of power is related to leadership because it is part of the influence process. Power is the capacity or potential to influence."[168]

"I guess that's why the Consultant wanted us to keep this morning's conversation in mind, since power and influence go hand in hand."

"True," the Receptionist said. "However, just because they go hand in hand, as you put it, doesn't mean they work together."

"What do you mean?" the account executive asked.

"Power might be involved in the influence process, but power can also be direct and without influence. You know, 'Do this because I said so, and I'm the boss.'"

"I see," he said. "So you believe power and influence are separate?"

"I don't know that they're separate necessarily, but I don't think they always work in tandem."

"I think what she's trying to say," I interjected, "is that in order for influence to occur, one must ascribe a certain amount of power to another. And if that is not the case, then power is wielded in the form of direct authority. Yes?"

She nodded. "Yes, something like that."

"All right," the account executive continued as he skimmed the file. "What you're referring to is *threat power*." He removed several copies of a document and passed them out to us. Then he read.

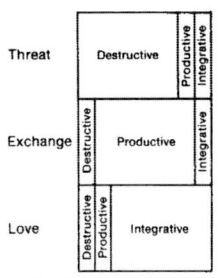

Figure 1.1. Categories of Power: Threat, Exchange, and Love

"Power can be divided 'into three categories from the point of view of its consequences: destructive power, productive power, and integrative power. Destructive power is the power to destroy things. Productive power is found in the fertilized egg, in the blueprint, in the idea, in the tools and machines that make things, in the activity of human brains, and muscles that sow and reap, weave and build, construct, paint, and sculpt. Integrative power may be thought of perhaps as an aspect of productive power that involves the capacity to build organizations, to create families and groups, to inspire loyalty, to bind people together, to develop legitimacy."[169]

He paused as we all studied the diagram.

The facilities manager commented, "It seems as though leadership power possesses, or can possess, all of those."

"Yeah," the shipping clerk added.

"Well," the account executive continued, "as we just mentioned, threat power is essentially, "You do something I want, or I will do something you do not want.""[170]

"We've all been there," the receptionist said snidely.

I wonder what that's all about, I thought.

"Don't you think that's necessary sometimes?" the facilities manager asked.

"No, I don't," she replied firmly. "I prefer to be asked, not threatened."

"Sometimes, there isn't time to ask," he said.

"What do you mean?" the account executive asked.

"I was in the navy. I gave orders, I didn't *ask* people to do things. The job has to get done, whether people want to do it or not. Sometimes it's necessary to threaten a person, which doesn't have to be direct. It can be implied via rank and the organizational structure. That's all I'm saying," he said with a tinge of anger in his voice.

"Okay," the account executive said. "I see what you're getting at, and I think you're right. Sometimes there is an implied threat due to position and structure." He paused and then continued reading, "Exchange power begins when A says to B, you do something I want, and I will do something you want."[171]

"Reciprocity," I said. "It's how things get done in an organization."

The shipping clerk smiled. "You call it reciprocity. I call it networking."

I smiled back. "Yes, I suppose you are right. Reciprocity is the foundation of successful networking, which brings up an interesting point regarding exchange power. It is voluntary. That is, each party has the option to act. To be successful, the individuals involved must be proactive."

"Very true," the facilities manager said. "I hate to belabor the point, but when I was in the military, I networked all the time. If I hadn't, it would have taken much longer for things to get done."[172]

"Great point," the account executive said. Then he continued, "In the love relationship, essentially, A says to B, 'You do something for me because you love me,' which could be a leader to a follower."[173]

"Wow!" the Receptionist said. "That could backfire."

"How so?" asked the account executive.

"It could become abusive, just like a dating relationship. One person takes advantage of the other because of the other's love or devotion."

"I see," he said, referring back to the folder. "What gives a leader power?" he asked.

"His or her position," the shipping clerk said.

"Not necessarily," the facilities manager said. "I knew people in leadership positions that no one would follow. They had very little power."

"The people give a leader his or her power," I said. "When we choose a leader we invest him [or her] with power, we listen to him [or her] because we, in our wisdom, have made him [or her] our leader."[174]

The account executive read from the document. "Power in organizations is a fluid social construction that is perceptual in nature, and that is subject to multiple interpretations."[175]

"What are the multiple interpretations?" asked the receptionist.

"Sources of power could be grouped into two broad categories, structural and behavioral,"[176] he read.

"Meaning," I added, "structural sources of power reflect the properties of a social system. Personal attributes and strategies constitute the behavioral sources of power."[177]

"Yes," the account executive said. "The leader who addresses the real needs of followers would have more power over followers."[178]

"True," I said. "Addressing the real needs of followers would have more power over followers,[179] which means, leadership needs a personal component."

"Leaders need to draw from the five power bases," the account executive added. He read from the document, "*Coercive power* is based on control over punishments. For example, suspensions, warnings, being excluded, and is used to secure compliance. *Legitimate power* stems from the follower's belief that the leader has the legitimate right and/or authority to influence, and that the follower is obliged to comply with the leader's orders. *Referent power* is based on the identification of the follower with the leader and on how much the follower likes, admires, respects, and wants to be like the leader. *Reward power* is nothing more than the ability to reward. *Expert power* is based on an accepted belief that the leader possesses skills and/or abilities that followers value and need."[180]

"How does a leader know which power base to draw upon?" the shipping clerk asked.

"Good question," the account executive said. "I suppose it depends on the situation and the person."

"I agree," I said. "Leadership is not plug and play. One side does not fit all. Leaders need to vary their approach."

"I suppose that's why leadership is so difficult," the shipping clerk said.

"Perhaps," the facilities manager said thoughtfully.

"If power is so necessary, why or how does it get abused?" the shipping clerk asked.

Oh, here we go, I thought.

The account executive removed a document from the folder. "As it just happens, the Consultant provided some information on that very topic.

"It is said that power corrupts, but more often than not, it is a corrupted individual who is attracted to power. It is a feeling of inferiority—sometimes called a Napoleon Complex—that drives someone to control other people and to micromanage their surroundings. Today, we call such a person a control freak. When we look at Abraham Maslow's hierarchy of human motivation (survival, safety, social, esteem, fulfillment), we see that someone who hungers for power is stuck in the second to bottom level, which is safety. A true leader has self-esteem and self-confidence and does not seek power to bolster his or her feeling of self-worth. Thomas Jefferson observed that an honest man can feel no pleasure in the exercise of power over his fellow citizens. A true leader is motivated by a goal—a goal common to his group, whether that group is a company or a country. If you find yourself attracted to leadership, stop and check your motivation. Are you driven to share your gift of understanding in the endeavor of achieving a goal or are you motivated by perquisites of position and the power you have over others? As John Quincy Adams said, 'If your actions inspire others to dream more, learn more, do more, and become more, you are a leader.'"[181]

"That certainly ties in with what we've studied this past week," I said. "One thing I've observed about power during my years in the business world is that abuse begins gradually. First, it's cutting a corner to save time. Then before you know it, someone is clearly crossing the line and acting like a loose cannon."

"Interesting point," the account executive said.

"So the real reason it happens is because it can, right?" the receptionist asked.

"Something like that," I said.

"I think it happens, because no one challenges a leader who appears to be doing something that benefits others, even if that means cutting corners or bending the rules," the facilities manager said. "It starts out with good intentions and then becomes the norm."

"Plus, like we discussed earlier this week, it becomes part of the organizational culture," the shipping clerk said.

"To a certain extent, I agree," the facilities manager said. "I think it becomes part of the subculture. That is, it's something that applies to a few, not the majority."

"I agree," I said. "I don't think there are too many organizations where the abuse of power runs rampant in all in individuals. Typically, from what I've experienced, it's limited to just a few."

We concluded our conversation, gathered our things, and headed out to lunch where the conversation about leadership and power continued.

Leadership Styles

"Well," the Consultant began, "this is our last group discussion of the week. We've covered a lot of material this week: values, ethics, morality, authentic leadership, integrity, leadership, and power. As we finish up this afternoon, we're going discuss different leadership styles and theories. After this discussion, you'll head into your last small group, where you'll remain and conduct your leadership application as well as prepare for your group presentation."

He wandered around the room as he continued to speak. "There are many theories about leadership, leaders, and their various styles. As you will see, each has merit." He paused in the center of the room and looked at a woman at table respect. "Suppose I offer to reward you if you change your behavior.

Let's imagine you're late every day, and I offer to give you a bonus if you can be on time. How does that sound?"

She smiled. "It sounds good to me. How much are we talking about?" Everyone laughed.

The Consultant said, "Well, the bonus could be letting you keep your job, or it could be monetary. It could go either way." He paused and let his words sink in. "That's an example of Transactional Leadership." He displayed a slide on the screen.

> ### TRANSACTIONAL LEADERSHIP
>
> Transactional leaders exchange things of value with subordinates to advance their own and their subordinates' agendas.
> Transactional leaders are influential because it is in the best interest of their subordinates to do what the leader wants.
>
> Peter Northouse, *Leadership: Theory and Practice* (California: Sage Publications, 2007), 185.

"Have any of you ever worked for a transactional leader?" the Consultant asked. There were a bunch of murmurs and a few groans. "I'll take that as a yes," he said with a smile. "Do you think this is common?"

"Yes," a member from table loyalty said. "It happens all the time. One hand washes the other."

"I see," the Consultant said. "Is that a good thing?"

"It can be," a woman from table respect said. "Transactional leadership builds the foundation for relationships between leaders and followers in terms of specifying expectations, clarifying responsibilities, negotiating contracts, and providing recognition and rewards in order to achieve the expected performance."[182]

"So it sets the tone, right?" the Consultant asked.

"Exactly," she said.

He nodded. "Very good. Moving on," he said. "Let's take a look at transformational leadership." He advanced the slide.

> ## TRANSFORMATIONAL LEADERSHIP
>
> Transformational leadership is a process that changes and transforms people. It is concerned with emotions, values, ethics, standards, and long-term goals and includes accessing followers' motives, satisfying their needs, and treating them as full human beings.
>
> Peter Northouse, Leadership: Theory and Practice (California: Sage Publications, 2007), 175.

"What are your thoughts about this?" he asked.

"I think it's the preferred method of leadership by followers," a gentleman from table compassion said.

"Why is that?" the Consultant asked.

"Because it is concerned more about progress and development, and it enhances the effects of transactional leadership,"[183] he responded.

"How does it do that?" he asked.

"It allows leaders to transform the personal values of followers to support the vision and goals of the organization by fostering an environment where relationships can be formed and by establishing a climate of trust in which visions can be shared."[184]

"So it's cooperative?" the Consultant asked.

"Definitely," he said.

"I see," the Consultant said. "And what about this?" he asked as he advanced the slide.

SITUATIONAL LEADERSHIP

Situational leadership stresses that leadership is composed of both a directive and supportive dimension, and each had to be applied appropriately in a given situation.

Peter Northouse, Leadership: Theory and Practice (California: Sage Publications, 2007), 91.

"That sounds kind of obvious to me," a man from table honesty said. "I believe it's true, but I also believe that it's a somewhat normal part of leadership development."

The Consultant displayed another slide. "This slide illustrates the concept and idea behind situational leadership." He then elaborated on the various components: directing, coaching, supporting, and delegating. In conclusion, he said, "Effectiveness is maximized by matching level of leadership style with follower readiness."[185]

A young girl at table trust said, "I think that's an interesting concept, and even though he"—she gestured at the man from *table honesty*—"thinks it's obvious, sometimes it's hard to tell someone's leadership level. I mean, some people give the impression they're at one level, when in reality, they're at another."

"And how do you handle that" the Consultant asked.

"Well, I downshift. That's how I think of it. I have to back-pedal."

"So what you really do is change your direction level, right?" he asked.

"Yes," she said.

"That's what this chart"—he motioned to the slide—"indicates."

Situational Leadership® II Model

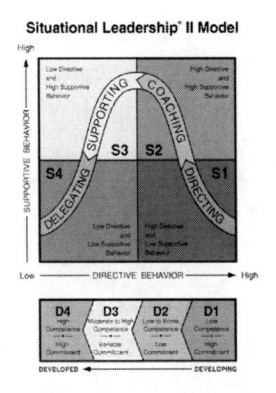

"Apply the right leadership style at the right time," a member from table compassion said.

"Exactly," the Consultant said. "The last leadership style we're going to discuss is the Leader-Member Exchange theory or LMX." He displayed another slide.

LMX

Leader-member exchange (LMX) theory describes the dyadic process by which a leader develops a relationship with each subordinate. The theory emphasizes that a leader's relationship often varies from one subordinate to another and that high quality LMX relationships are developed with some subordinates whereas low quality LMX relationships are developed with other subordinates.

O'Donnell, Mark, Gary Yukl, and Thomas Taber. "Leader Behavior and LMX: A Constructive Replication." Journal of Managerial Psychology 27, no. 2 (2012): 143.

"Many people relate to this theory because of the relationship experiences they've had within an organization," he said. "What are your thoughts?"

"It seems as though this is a more personalized style of leadership," I said.

"True," he said. "Subordinates become a part of the in-group or out-group, based on how well they work with the leaders and how well the leader works with them.[186] But what about those individuals who aren't included such a relationship?"

"Well," I began, "it seems subordinates in the in-group [would be more likely] to receive more information, influence, confidence, and concern from their leaders than out-group subordinates."[187]

"Yes," he said. "That is very true. In fact, in-group members would be more likely to go above and beyond for their leader, while out-group members will typically just come to work, do their job, and go home."[188] He began to walk around the room. "Now that we've examined and discussed some leadership styles and theories, let's consider them in regard to values and ethical behavior. Do you believe one style or theory is more likely to produce strong values and ethical behavior over another, and if so, why?" His question hung in the air, as we all considered it.

"I'll take a stab at it," a man from my table said. "Organizations dominated by unethical climates may create a breeding ground for the emergence of specific negative individual effects[189] that could be enhanced through leader-follower relationship, such as LMX or situational leadership."

"So instead of fostering a positive climate that reinforces positive values and ethical behavior, leadership styles that depend on relationships could have the opposite effect?" he asked.

"Yes."

He nodded. "Okay, what else?"

"It seems to me transactional leadership could easily produce unethical behavior in others," I said. "Transactional leaders are primarily concerned with managing outcomes and seeking behavioral compliance with practices that will maximize the mutual interests of both parties.[190] So if either the leader or the followers have a tendency to behave unethically, they could easily go down the wrong path and be rewarded for doing so."

"Excellent," he said. "What about transformational leadership?" I was beginning to see how everything we covered this week was starting to come full circle.

"I think transactional leaders are more inclined to moral behavior," a young man at table loyalty said. "I think, transformational leaders center their influence process on changing followers' core attitudes and values so that they are consistent with the vision for the organization. The transformational influence process is predicated on the norm of social responsibility.[191] As such, I imagine there is less chance of unethical behavior."

"Very good," the Consultant said. "Leadership style can have a significant impact on a follower's behavior, and it can be a tremendous influence when it comes to expected behavior." He wandered back to the podium and advanced the slide. "One more theory of leadership we are going to discuss is *servant leadership*."

> ### SERVANT LEADERSHIP
>
> "The servant-leader *is* servant first... It begins with the natural feeling that one wants to serve, to serve *first*. Then conscious choice brings one to aspire to lead."
>
> Robert Greenleaf, "What is Servant Leadership," https://greenleaf.org/what-is-servant-leadership/

"Servant leadership is a leadership theory that was made popular by Robert Greenleaf," he said. "Has anyone ever worked for a servant leader?"

A woman at table loyalty shot her hand up. "I did, many years ago, and it was a wonderful experience."

"Why was that?" he asked.

"Well, she was a younger woman, and I had my doubts about her before I began working for her but she always took care of everyone on her staff. She made me feel like she worked for me."

"I see," he said. "That is vey empowering." He turned to the group. "Other thoughts?"

"A servant leader's first concern is with the growth of others, not the self. That basic concept would go a long way toward developing more ethical leadership,"[192] a man from table honesty said.

"Excellent," the Consultant said. "Great point. Does anyone else believe servant leadership is more inclined to promote ethical behavior?"

"Yes," a woman from table respect said. "Ethical leaders develop their followers by modeling behavior [they] frequently communicate with their followers about ethics, set clear ethical standards, and use rewards and punishments to see that those standards are followed,[193] he said. More importantly, ethical leaders do not just talk a good game, they practice what they preach and are proactive role models for ethical conduct."

"Excellent," he said. "Do you think you can teach servant leadership?"

A man at table compassion said, "Servant leadership can be taught to [individuals] as a significant part of ethics education and can also be developed in organizations as a way to improve the ethical climate of the business."[194]

"I see said," the Consultant said. "How can it be taught?"

The man replied, "It can be taught to individual[s] as a foundation for character that will enable them to resist negative corporate pressures. It can also be taught to organizations to make both the organization and the individuals within the organization more ethical."[195]

"So we're back to character now?" the Consultant asked. The man just nodded. "Good," he said. "In a few minutes, you will attend your last small group discussion of the program. You are going to discuss leadership differences between men and women. After which, you will develop your daily leadership application. Additionally, you will have time to work on your group presentations."

With that, we gathered our things and headed to the conference room.

This should be an interesting topic, I thought. When he announced the topic, I realized all the groups were comprised of men and women. *He thought of everything*, I mused to myself.

Men versus Women

It was the shipping clerk's second time leading the group. This discussion was going to be a bit shorter than the others so we would have time to prepare for the group presentation that would follow. The shipping clerk appeared a bit nervous, probably because of the topic.

"Okay," he said. "Last small group meeting of the week. We're going to discuss some of the differences between men and women, when it comes to leadership."

"Listen," I said, hoping to put him at ease, "it's a topic like any other. We'll just discuss it based on the instructions, okay?" I smiled.

"Yes," he said, an air of relief washing over him. He glanced down at the folder. "Who make better leaders, men or women?" he asked.

"Women, of course," I smiled.

"Yeah," the receptionist said, giving me a high five. The men just laughed.

"This is going to be a loaded discussion," the facilities manager said.

"Yup," the account executive added. After a brief pause, he said, "I guess it depends on his or her effectiveness. I don't think it's purely a gender thing."

"I agree," I said. "Quantifying which gender is the better leader has to be based on some sort of measurable standard. 'Leadership effectiveness is measured using numerous indicators, such as followers' attitudes, level of commitment given to the organization, and motivation towards the job."[196]

"Agreed," the account executive said. "Another indicator determining the effectiveness of leadership is the performance and outcomes of the organization or of group productivity. Leaders are often perceived to be effective when an organization achieves high profitability and productivity."[197]

"Yeah, it's all about money," the receptionist said.

"Female CEOs are on the rise," I said. "I'll admit, I was surprised when I was offered the job, but I quickly realized nearly seventy-three percent of Fortune 500 companies now have at least one female executive officer."[198]

"Really?" the account executive said. "That's impressive."

"Yes," I said, nodding.

"Okay," the shipping clerk said, getting us back on track. "So who wants power more, men or women?"

"Men!" the Receptionist stated emphatically.

"Oh? And why is that?" the facilities manager asked.

"Because it's a man's world," she stated with disdain.

"Oh, is it?" he said.

I jumped in. "I think women want power just as much as men, if not more."

"Why?" the account executive asked.

"Well, women are still coming into their own in corporate America, so to speak, so it seems they would be more motivated to get ahead and prove themselves. Women want power more than men do because they feel they can make a positive contribution to the organization[199] and need the requisite power to do that."

"I can see that," the facilities manager said. "I think it really depends on the person."

"Me too," the shipping clerk said.

"It also depends on their motivation," the receptionist said.

"Yes," I agreed, "specifically, power motivation."

"What's that?" she asked.

"Power motivation [is] defined as an interpersonal difference in the desire to influence others,"[200] I said.

"Oh," was all she managed.

"Yes," the account executive said. "Women have been found to be more interpersonally oriented, more task-oriented, more democratic, and more transformational than men overall."[201]

"That's interesting," she said. "Does that make them better leaders?"

"I don't know about that," he said. "I think women bring a different dynamic to leadership than men. It's not necessarily better, just different, and together, men and women can lead cooperatively," the account executive said.

"Let me ask you this," the facilities manager said as he looked at me. "You're the CEO. What's your power motivation? You climbed the company ladder, so to speak. How do you feel about power?"

I thought for a moment. "Well, I never really thought about it. I've always been an extrovert. My parents raised me to be an independent woman. They told me I could do anything a man could do and to never give up." I paused as I considered his questions. "I wasn't expecting this job when I got it, so getting it wasn't a matter of power for me. I guess you could say, my power motivation is to make the Company the best it can be."

The shipping clerk consulted the file and smiled. "Okay," he said. "Here is something you"—he gestured toward me—"might find interesting. Women assuming senior leadership positions literally bring change. When a woman is visibly chosen to become president, prime minister, or CEO when no other woman has ever held such an office and when few people thought she would be selected, other major organizational and societal changes become believably possible."[202]

Nothing like being put on the spot, I thought. *The Consultant really set me up for this one.* "Well," I began, "I guess I should comment. As the first female CEO in the Company's history, my presence is certainly a change for many. Like I said, I was surprised when I was offered the position. I wasn't even seeking it. However, after being at the helm for a few months, I can honestly say I enjoy the job. It's very challenging—very," I said with a slight laugh. Everyone laughed in acknowledgement of my subtle reference to the debacles that had recently plagued the Company.

The shipping clerk pulled five copies of a handout from the folder and passed them out. "This is from an article in *Forbes* regarding the leadership traits of women," he said.

1. Opportunity-driven

When confronted with a challenge, the women I know look for the opportunity within. They see the glass as half-full rather than half-empty. They push the boundaries and, when faced with adverse circumstances, they learn all they can from it. Optimism is their mindset because they see opportunity in everything.

2. Strategic

Women see what often times others don't see. As one of my women mentors told me, "A woman's lens of skepticism oftentimes forces them to see well beyond the most obvious details before them. They enjoy stretching their perspective to broaden their observations. Many women are not hesitant to peel the onion in order to get to the root of the matter."

3. Passionate

While women in general were historically viewed and stereotyped as emotional leaders by men, I believe they are just passionate explorers in pursuit of excellence. When women leaders are not satisfied with the status quo, they will want to make things better. These women leaders get things done and avoid procrastination. As another one of my women mentors said, "They enjoy order and stability and a genuine sense of control. Many women have learned not to depend upon others for their advancement and thus have a tendency to be too independent. A woman's independent nature is her way of finding her focus and dialing up her pursuits."

4. Entrepreneurial

Entrepreneurship is just a way of life for many women. They can be extremely resourceful, connect the dots of opportunity and become expert in developing the relationships they need to get the job done. Many women leaders also see through an entrepreneurial lens to best enable the opportunities before them. They know that to create and sustain momentum requires 100% focus on the objective—and so they don't enjoy being disrupted by unnecessary noise and distractions.

5. Purposeful and Meaningful

I have found that many women leaders enjoy inspiring others to achieve. They know what it's like to be the underdog and work hard not to disappoint themselves and others. Women leaders in particular often have high standards and their attention to detail makes it difficult for others to cut corners or abuse any special

6. Traditions and Family

> Whether at home or at work, women are often the glue that keeps things together and that is why they represent great leadership for America's future. When they sense growing tensions that can lead to potential problems or inefficiencies, the most successful women leaders enjoy taking charge before circumstances force their hand. Women are usually the ones to secure the foundational roots of the family and to protect family and cultural traditions from wavering.[203]

The account executive said, "I think, this demonstrates what I said earlier that women bring a different perspective to leadership. I think it's definitely an advantage to have a mix of male and female leaders in an organization."

"I agree," I smiled. "I don't think it's a matter of who's the better leader. I think it's a matter of harnessing strengths."

"Me too," the receptionist said.

The shipping clerk looked through the folder and said, "Well, that pretty much wraps it up. We can do our leadership application and work on our presentation." He pulled a copy of a Power Point out of the folder and placed it on the table.

Leadership Application

> **LEADERSHIP APPLICATION**
>
> - What is the issue?
> - What are the implications for The Company?
> - Why does it matter?
> - How can The Company promote the effective use of power by its leaders?
> - If leaders implemented different styles, what would be the impact for The Company?

We quickly got down to business and answered the questions. We wanted to have as much time as possible to finalize our group presentations. The receptionist recorded our answers.

1. The issue is that power unchecked can lead to abuse.
2. As we have already seen, the abuse of power can lead to mistreatment and unwanted incidents.
3. This matters because these types of incidents can permanently damage the culture of a company and its leaders.
4. Power can be kept in check via leadership styles and organizational culture.

5. If leaders utilized different leadership styles, the culture might improve and employee happiness and effectiveness.

Group Presentations

The Consultant had provided instructions for our group presentations at the beginning of the week. They were very simple. In addition to our daily leadership applications, we were to consider the Company's values, in light of the training, and present a plan to increase awareness of those values.

Only one of us was required to speak; however, everyone was required to participate in the process. You'll never who was elected to speak for my group! I didn't mind. In some ways, it was fitting and a little expected.

We were only given five minutes for the presentation and three additional minutes available for questions. The Consultant would keep track of the time. For our presentation, we reviewed our leadership applications and decided on a simple strategy.

I stood behind the podium and introduced the members of my group. "Being the CEO and making this presentation carries an implied obligation, I suppose," I said with a smile. Everyone, including the Consultant, laughed. "My group and I came up with the idea of promoting awareness of the Company's core values via a committee that would conduct regular training and events designed to reinforce our values (integrity, loyalty, and service) and what they mean to us. One idea we had was to internalize the Company's values. That is, redirect them to improve our culture, and in some cases, change it. What became clear to us through our discussion was that oftentimes, core values are assumed to apply externally to our clients."

I paused for a moment as I surveyed the room. I had everyone's attention. "We are clients to each other. We lead one another, follow one another, and must serve each other's needs if we are going to remain relevant and successful. Our daily interactions with one another must reflect our core values if they are to have meaning to who we are and what we do." I saw the Consultant in the back of the room inconspicuously pointing to his watch. "Thank you," I said. "Does anyone have any questions?"

Either, I had shocked them with what I said or no one wanted to rock the boat, but no one had any questions so I took my seat and listened to the other tables give their presentations. There were many good ideas—some of which I wrote down. I was going to implement them after everyone had been through the training.

Leadership Application

As was our custom throughout the week, the Consultant met me in my office after training. "That was great training," I said. "It's obvious you've given it many times." I smiled.

"What do you mean?" he asked, genuinely puzzled.

"I mean, you were very familiar with the content and its delivery. Obviously, because you've taught that curriculum on previous occasions."

It was his turn to smile. "Cheryl, that was the first time I taught that curriculum."

"What? Are you kidding me?" I asked. "No way."

"Yes," he said.

"I don't get it. You mean, you designed and developed that entire program just for the Company?"

"Yes, Cheryl. I'm a consultant. That's what I do."

"But how?" I continued.

"That's why I spent so much time talking with everyone after we first met. You can't conduct training if you don't know the need." He winked with a smile.

Wow! I thought. *Custom-made training. What a concept!*

EPILOGUE

A true leader has the confidence to stand alone, the courage to make tough decisions, and the compassion to listen to the needs of others. He does not set out to be a leader, but becomes one by the equality of his actions and the integrity of his intent.

—Douglas MacArthur

Ironically, as I was straightening some papers on my desk, I came across the report the Consultant had provided. I was scheduled to meet with him this morning. It had been three months since everyone at the Company had attended the Leadership Academy. When we were finished, the Consultant told me it would take time to change our culture. Even so, I noticed some changes right away. I started to thumb through the report and began to read it again.

Introduction

At The Company's request, the Bishop Advisory Group was retained to assess The Company's culture and conduct a Values

Assessment Survey. The following report is an analysis of The Company for the period specified. The Organizational Culture Assessment Instrument and Values Assessment Survey was used in conjunction with personnel interviews and direct observations to collect and aggregate data about The Company's organizational culture and core values.

Objective

The objective of this consulting report is to identify the culture of The Company, assess its core values awareness and their effectiveness, and communicate and observe its personnel in order to formulate appropriate recommendations that will create awareness and provide a specific plan that will meet its future cultural planning needs as it relates to leadership and organizational theory.

The completion of this analysis included the following methods:

- *Organizational Culture Assessment Instrument (OCAI)*
- *Values Assessment Survey*
- *Personnel interviews*
- *Direct observations*

Key Issues:
OCAI

- **Dominant Characteristics:**
  (Now) The OCAI revealed The Company is results-oriented and is focused on getting the job done. Personnel are very competitive and view the command as very structured.
  (Preferred) The Company is preferred to be a personal place where people share a lot of themselves.

- **Organizational Leadership:**
  (Now) The Company leadership is straightforward and is primarily concerned with getting the job done. There is little or no room for risk taking or mentoring.
  (Preferred) Personnel would like the organization to adopt a culture of facilitating, mentoring, and nurturing.

- **Management of Employees:**
  (Now) The Company is characterized by a sense of teamwork and universal participation mixed with fair amount of competitiveness.
  (Preferred) Personnel would like to have more autonomy to innovate and take risks.

- ***Organization Glue:***
  (Now) *Goal accomplishment and achievement coupled with a strong desire to win and excel are the glue that holds The Company together.*
  (Preferred) *Loyalty, trust, and commitment are preferred as the organizational glue.*

- ***Strategic Emphasis:***
  (Now) *Personnel believe The Company emphasizes competition and achievement in order to achieve goals.*
  (Preferred) *The preferred emphasis is to transform The Company into an organization of high trust, openness, and participation.*

- ***Criteria for Success:***
  (Now) *The Company defines success based on winning and competition.*
  (Preferred) *Personnel would like the organization to define success on the basis of human resource development, teamwork, and employee commitment.*

Values Assessment

- *The majority of Company personnel do not know its core values, nor do they know its mission statement.*
- *Unethical practices were identified.*
- *Company personnel believe unethical behavior is contagious.*
- *Strong values are critical to organizational success.*

Personnel Interviews and Observations

- *Favoritism is perceived to be systemic in many departments.*
- *Privilege is granted to those who occupy management positions.*
- *Above-the-law mentality exists at the senior management level.*
- *Protection and support by The Company is believed to be an inherent right by senior personnel.*

Analysis

The six dimensions of organizational culture assessed by OCAI indicate The Company has a market culture. Market-type organizations are characterized by competitiveness and productivity, which is conducive to success in an organization that is based on serving the needs of the fleet. Due to the nature of The Company's mission, it is not surprising that the OCAI revealed a results-driven work environment. In a business where winning translates into living or dying, the market culture emphasizes winning amidst competitive actions and goal completion.[204]

The OCAI revealed the preferred culture was a Clan. That is, personnel would like to work in a collaborative environment. Clan cultures are based on a high level of teamwork and a friendly work environment akin to a big family. They thrive on loyalty and trust and promote the expression of opinions and ideas. Often such organizations have a high commitment level amongst employees.[205]

Strengths

The market culture serves the needs of the employees and the organization well. Productivity is the mainstay of The Company and is the reason for its very existence. Providing fast, reliable service to its customers is the epitome of its mission. The demand and drive by management to increase productivity while decreasing costs has created an environment where winning is everything. Winning in this particular environment is defined as effecting repairs and performing preventative maintenance that renders seagoing units capable of completing their assigned missions without delay.

Weaknesses

The market culture stimulates an environment where competition and the desire to win supersede the importance of the individual. Collaboration is not so much discouraged as it is prevented by the overwhelming desire to win at any cost. Management has little time or inclination to listen to the opinions and ideas of others regardless of their relevance. Rather, management operates on the assumption that "a clear purpose and an aggressive strategy lead to productivity and profitability."[206] This perspective may provide a secure customer base, but it leaves little room for teamwork.

Recommendations

The following recommendations are made to move the command toward a Clan culture:

1. *Institute an effective employee survey program for systematically monitoring employee attitudes and ideas. The Company utilizes the annual climate survey to assess the perceived climate of the command. This is mandated by regulation and is rigidly constructed by the Navy as a whole. While it allows for some tailoring of individual questions, the survey is broad in scope and application. Using an internally developed survey on a recurring basis, i.e. monthly, will provide more relevant and timely information about attitudes and ideas. It will promote an environment of teamwork. Increase attendance in training programs. Training programs at a government, technical organization are ubiquitous. Often absent, though, are supervisors, who 'opt out' of training in lieu of having more pressing matters to which to attend. Mandating supervisors attend training will create an atmosphere of equality and boost the level of trust between subordinates and supervisors.*
2. *Increase the effectiveness of the employee suggestion box. The suggestion box is often the not-so-anonymous complaint box. As such, it is infrequently utilized for its intended purpose. Providing anonymity and a viable outlet for suggestions coupled with an effective recognition system will foster an open and friendly environment.*
3. *Energize the employee recognition system. Employees are typically recognized at the conclusion of mandatory meet-*

ings with little fanfare. Acknowledging employee contributions with vigor, enthusiasm, and genuine appreciation will promote long-term human resource development and lay the foundation for a collaborative culture.

The following recommendations are made to increase core values awareness and promote ethical behavior:

1. *Conduct integrative, organizational training on values and ethics for all personnel.*
2. *Revamp The Company's core values to reflect those identified by Company personnel via training.*
3. *Harness the power of social media by introducing a values campaign.*
4. *Promote open parking for all employees in order to diminish the culture of elitism.*
5. *Incorporate Company training program on values and ethics as part of the on-boarding process.*

Conclusion

The Company operates in a Market culture. This promotes competition and an atmosphere that emphasizes winning. The preferred culture is that of a Clan, where collaboration and teamwork embody the organization. Through the utilization of surveys and enhanced recognition systems, The Company can progress toward an organizational culture that values human resource development and fosters loyalty and trust.

The Consultant had certainly delivered. After the training was completed for all personnel, I called Robert to thank him for recommending him. My intercom buzzed and my secretary informed me the Consultant had arrived.

He strode into the office, smiled, and extended his hand. "Cheryl, it's good to see you again," he said warmly as I shook his hand.

I walked around the desk and sat opposite him in the twin chairs in front of my desk. "It's good to see you too."

"How are things?" he asked.

"Things are definitely improving. I've noticed a discernable change in the culture, which, I'm sure, is due to the values campaign and challenge," I said.

The values challenge was one his recommendations in which employees posted short videos of themselves on the Company's Facebook page. In the videos, employees stated their name, position, time with the Company, and held up a piece of paper with a handwritten value they believed was the most important. They then explained why that value was important to them and challenged three other employees to do the same. Ironically, the Consultant suggested I start the campaign, so I did. I called out two board members and a senior vice president—and so, the process had begun. Within less than a month, every employee had posted a video. People were logging into Facebook several times a day—including me—to see who had posted.

In my video, I held up a sheet of paper on which I had written *integrity*. I said, "Hello, I'm Cheryl Stevens, CEO. I've been with the company for six years, and my value is integrity. Integrity is who you are all the time, at home and at work. It defines you as a person and a leader. Your integrity must be beyond reproach."

"I see you are wearing your values button," he observed. He was referring the button on my blazer, which said *integrity* in bold letters against the Company's logo. Part of the values campaign was to have buttons made with all the values identified by the employees at the training sessions. When the shipment arrived, we all met in the employee cafeteria, and I handed them out to everyone after a catered lunch. The values campaign committee did a terrific job planning the event. It was a smashing success, and I said so to the Consultant.

"That is great to hear," he said. "I am so happy for you and the Company."

"Thank you," I said sincerely. "For everything."

"You are very welcome," he said genuinely. After a brief pause, he said, "I brought a sample of the training materials." He opened his briefcase and removed a binder, book, and CD. "The student guides and Power Points are on the disk," he said. "This"—he held up the binder—"is the facilitator's guide." I opened it and paged through it. As I did, he explained, "I'll provide a train-the-trainer session for your training department. Also, there are train-the-trainer module videos on the disk that can be used for future reference by the training department."

"Great," I said. "This is really going to make a difference and add value to our onboarding process." As part of his recommendations, the Consultant advised training members of the Company's training department to deliver the values program we had all taken as part of our onboarding process. He believed this would add buy-in, especially in light of the values campaign. I agreed and accepted his offer to conduct train-the-trainer sessions and certify members of the training department to teach his curriculum.

"And this," he said, handing me a copy of his book that would serve as the textbook for the program, "is your personal copy."

I read the title to myself, *The Currency of Leadership* by Dr. William H. Bishop. I opened it and smiled as I read his fitting inscription.

> *To Cheryl –*
>
> *To lead effectively, your integrity must be beyond reproach. The currency of leadership is comprised of your values, behavior, and integrity. Be the leader your followers need you to be, your authentic self!*
>
> *Bill*

AFTERWORD

I trust this story has been both entertaining and informative. You might be wondering to yourself, *Now what? Where do I go from here?* Well, there is no one-size-fits-all answer. Leadership is a complex undertaking that requires constant effort to improve. When it comes to values, character, and integrity, leaders must seek new experiences and embrace challenge in order to test their mettle. The lessons of leadership are forged through experiences, both good and bad. It is through these experiences that a leader develops his character, which is why many believe leaders are made and not born.

As this story has depicted, changing your values is akin to changing your identity. A daunting task to be sure, but it can be done. Your values are uniquely linked to who you are. They are based on your experiences and beliefs and are influenced by family, friends, mentors, society, and culture. In many ways, they make you the person you are. However, values are perpetually evolving. As we grow older, we change our opinions and develop new perspectives. Why does this happen? It happens because we are teachable creatures. We are constantly adapting and learning. Life events, such as marriage, divorce, children, etc., contribute to the formation of our values and the importance we place upon them. Changes within an organization—promotions, merges, new policies, tasks, and assignments—contribute to values development and integration, which is why leaders need to know the pulse of their organization. They must be engaged on a daily basis. Leaders must have meaningful interactions that reflect core values.

Where you go from here is the mirror. Take a long, hard look at what you see. Ask yourself, *Who am I? What kind of leader do I want to be? What are my values and do I reflect them everyday?* If you really want a humbling experience, ask your people what they think about your leadership ability. Chances are, you won't hear anything disparaging—at least, not the first few times you ask. But keep at it. Hold regular meetings, where you allow your people to assess your performance. Don't get defensive; just listen. If your people are right—and you'll know if they are, because their comments will really hit home—acknowledge they are right. Then humble yourself and ask for their assistance. Solicit suggestions on how you can improve. Don't just listen to what they tell you; apply their suggestions. You must be willing to improve. Sometimes, the only way to do that is by submitting yourself to others. "As iron sharpens iron, so one person sharpens another," (Prov. 27:17, NIV). And so it is with leadership.

NOTES

Preface

1. Ronald R. Sims and Johannes Brinkmann, "Enron Ethics (Or: Culture Matters More than Codes)." *Journal of Business Ethics* 45, no. 3 (07, 2003), 249.
2. Jean Folger, "The Enron Collapse: A Look Back," *Investopedia* (December 1, 2011) http://www.investopedia.com/financial-edge/1211/the-enron-collapse-a-look-back.aspx.
3. Mclean, Bethany and Joe Nocera, *All the Devils Are Here* (New York: Penguin Publishing Group, 2010), 130.
4. Gregory Curtis, *The Financial Crisis and the Collapse of Ethical Behavior* (2008) http://www.now-andfutures.com/d2/ethics_and_integrity_issues_were_the_cause_WhitePaper044-FinancialCrisis.pdf.

Chapter 1

5. Damodar Suar and Rooplekha Khuntia, "Influence of Personal Values and Value Congruence on Unethical Practices and Work Behavior." *Journal of Business Ethics* 97, no. 3 (2010), 443.
6. Miltion Rokeach, *The Nature of Human Values.* Accesses June 27, 2014, 7. https://www.uzh.ch/cmsssl/suz/albert/lehre/wertewandel2011/B01_Rokeach1973.pdf
7. William Hitt, *Ethics and Leadership: Putting Theory into Practice.* (Columbus, OH: Battelle Press, 1990), 28.
8. Frank Navran, "Defining Values, Morals, and Ethics," *Navran Associates,* www.navran.com/article-values-morals-ethics.html.
9. Margaret Lindorff, "The Personal Values of Tomorrow's Workforce: Similarities and Differences Across Sex and Nationality." *Journal of Management and Organization* 16, no. 3 (07, 2010): 353–368. http://0-search.proquest.com.library.regent.edu/docview/748836726?accountid=13479.
10. Barry Z. Posner, "Another Look at the Impact of Personal and Organizational Values Congruency." *Journal of Business Ethics* 97, no. 4 (12, 2010), 536.
11. Carl A. Kogut, Larry E. Short, and Jerry L. Wall, "Personal Values: What are They Worth?" *Allied Academies International Conference. Academy for*

Economics and Economic Education. Proceedings 12, no. 1 (2009), 7.

12. Raymond Boudon, *The Origin of Values: Sociology and Philosophy of Beliefs.* (New Jersey: Transaction Publishers, 2001), 2.

13. Steven Hitlin and Jane Allyn Piliavin, "Values: Reviving a Dormant Concept." *Annual Review of Sociology* 30, (2004), 383.

14. Anna Doring, Andrea Blauensteiner, Katrin Aryus, Lisa Drogekamp, and Wolfgang Blisky, "Assessing Values at an Early Age: The Picture-Based Value Survey for Children (PBVS-C)." *Journal Of Personality Assessment* 92, no. 5 (2010), 443.

15. Hans Joas, *The Genesis of Values.* (Chicago, IL: University of Chicago Press, 2000), 1.

16. Jan Cieciuch and Shalom H. Schwartz, "The Number of Distinct Basic Values and Their Structure Assessed by PVQ–40." *Journal Of Personality Assessment* 94, no. 3 (2012), 321.

17. Miltion Rokeach, *The Nature of Human Values.* Accesses June 27, 2014, 20. https://www.uzh.ch/cmsssl/suz/albert/lehre/wertewandel2011/B01_Rokeach1973.pdf

18. Patrick Gambrel and Rebecca Cianci, "Maslow's hierarchy of needs: Does it Apply in a Collectivist Culture." *Journal of Applied Management and Entrepreneurship* 8, no. 2 (2003), 149.

19. Patrick Gambrel and Rebecca Cianci, "Maslow's hierarchy of needs: Does it Apply in a Collectivist Culture." *Journal of Applied Management and Entrepreneurship* 8, no. 2 (2003), 150.
20. Miltion Rokeach, *The Nature of Human Values.* Accesses June 27, 2014, 3. https://www.uzh.ch/cmsssl/suz/albert/lehre/wertewandel2011/B01_Rokeach1973.pdf
21. Nina Kiovula, *Basic Human Values in the Workplace.* (2008), 9. https://helda.helsinki.fi/bitstream/handle/10138/23465/basichum.pdf?sequence=2 (accessed June 30, 2014).
22. Nina Kiovula, *Basic Human Values in the Workplace.* (2008), 38–39.
23. Organizational Cultural Assessment Instrument (May 10, 2010) http://www.uiowa.edu/~nrcfcp/dmcrc/documents/OCAIProExampleReport.pdf.
24. Ibid.
25. Kim Cameron and Robert Quinn, *Diagnosing and Changing Organizational Culture Based on the Competing Values Framework.* (California: Jossey-Bass, 2011), 44.
26. William H. Bishop, "The Necessity of Unification in Globalization," *Leadership Advance Online,* XXV, (2014), 4.
27. Robert House, Paul Hanges, Mansour Javidan, Peter Dorfman, and Vipin Gupta, *Culture, Lead-*

ership, and Organizations: The GLOBE Study of 62 Societies. (Thousand Oaks, CA: Sage Publications, 2004), 15.

28. Mansour Javidan, Robert J. House, Peter W. Dorfman, Paul J. Hanges, and Sully de Luque, "Conceptualizing and Measuring Cultures and their Consequences: A Comparative Review of GLOBE's and Hofstede's Approaches." *Journal of International Business Studies* 37, no. 6 (2006), 899.

29. Mansour Javidan, Robert J. House, Peter W. Dorfman, Paul J. Hanges, and Sully de Luque, "Conceptualizing and Measuring Cultures and their Consequences: A Comparative Review of GLOBE's and Hofstede's Approaches." *Journal of International Business Studies* 37, no. 6 (2006), 899.

30. Patrick Gambrel and Rebecca Cianci, "Maslow's hierarchy of needs: Does it Apply in a Collectivist Culture." *Journal of Applied Management and Entrepreneurship* 8, no. 2 (2003), 146.

31. Patrick Gambrel and Rebecca Cianci, "Maslow's hierarchy of needs: Does it Apply in a Collectivist Culture." *Journal of Applied Management and Entrepreneurship* 8, no. 2 (2003), 146.

32. Ping Ping Fu, Jeff Kennedy, Jasmine Tata, Gary Yukl, Harris Bond Michael, Tai-Kuang Peng, Ekkirala S. Srinivas, et al., "The Impact of Societal Cultural Values and Individual Social Beliefs on

the Perceived Effectiveness of Managerial Influence Strategies: A Meso Approach." *Journal of International Business Studies* 35, no. 4 (2004), 285.
33. Paul Brewer and Sunil Venaik, "Individualism-Collectivism in Hofstede and GLOBE." *Journal of International Business Studies* 42, no. 3 (04, 2011), 438.
34. Maria Rosario Gonzalez-Rodriguez, Maria Carmen Diaz-Fernandez, and Simonetti Biagio, "Values and Corporate Social Initiative: An Approach Through Schwartz Theory." *International Journal of Business and Society* (2014), 15, no. 1, 20.
35. Maria Rosario Gonzalez-Rodriguez, Maria Carmen Diaz-Fernandez, and Simonetti Biagio, "Values and Corporate Social Initiative: An Approach Through Schwartz Theory." *International Journal of Business and Society* (2014), 15, no. 1, 22.
36. Nina Kiovula, *Basic Human Values in the Workplace.* (2008). https://helda.helsinki.fi/bitstream/handle/10138/23465/basichum.pdf?sequence=2 (accessed June 30, 2014).
37. Nina Kiovula, *Basic Human Values in the Workplace.* (2008). https://helda.helsinki.fi/bitstream/handle/10138/23465/basichum.pdf?sequence=2 (accessed June 30, 2014).
38. David Kim, Dan Fisher, and David McCalman, "Modernism, Christianity, and Business Ethics: A

Worldview Perspective." *Journal of Business Ethics* 90, no. 1 (11, 2009), 116.

39. Hector Falcon, "Exploring the Motivating Factors that Contributed to the Founding of a Biblical Worldview Leadership Training Organization: A Phenomenological Study of an Entrepreneur," (2007), 3.
40. Sasha Goldstein, "Aryan Brotherhood Targeting Black Teens Who Beat WWII Vet To Death: Cops," *Daily News,* November 21, 2013, Accessed June 27, 2014. http://www.nydailynews.com/news/crime/aryan-brotherhood-targeting-black-teens-beat-wii-vet-death-cops-article-1.1525396
41. *Aryan Brotherhood*, directed by Kathleen Cromley (United States: National Geographic, 2007), DVD.
42. Ibid.
43. Ibid.
44. Ibid.
45. Ibid.
46. Ibid.
47. Deborah Laible, Jessica Eye, and Gustavo Carlo, 2008. "Dimensions of Conscience in Mid-Adolescence: Links with Social Behavior, Parenting, and Temperament." *Journal of Youth and Adolescence* (2008), 37, no 7, 875.
48. Ibid.

49. Nico P. Swartz and Obonye Jonas, "The Superiority or Integrity of Natural Law for Our Time." *International Law Research* 1, no. 1 (2012): 119–129.
50. Kevin E. O'Reilly, 2014. "The Church as the Defender of Conscience in Our Age." *Nova Et Vetera (English Edition)* 12, no. 1: 193–215. *Academic Search Complete*, EBSCO*host* (accessed June 28, 2014), 200.
51. Annie Reiner, 2009. *The Quest for Conscience and the Birth of the Mind*. London: Karnac Books, 2009. *eBook Collection (EBSCOhost)*, EBSCO*host* (accessed June 28, 2014), 49.
52. G. Vithoulkas and D. F. Muresanu, "Conscience and Consciousness: a definition." *Journal of Medicine & Life* 7, no. 1 (January 2014), 105.
53. William Lyons, "Conscience—an Essay in Moral Psychology." *Philosophy* 84, no. 4 (10, 2009), 493.
54. Tom Beauchamp and Norman Bowie, *Ethical Theory and Business* (New Jersey: Pearson Education, Inc., 2004), 6.
55. William Lyons, "Conscience—an Essay in Moral Psychology." *Philosophy* 84, no. 4 (10, 2009), 481.
56. Jan Klos, "Spontaneous Order Versus Organized Order." *Journal of Markets and Morality* 6, no. 1 (2003), 171.

57. Peg Tittle, *Critical Thinking: An Appeal to Reason.* New York: Routledge, 2011, 4.
58. Ibid, 9.

Chapter Two

59. William Hitt, *Ethics and Leadership: Putting Theory into Practice* (Ohio: Battelle Memorial Institute, 1990), 56.
60. "Ethics and Morality," *Chapter 7,* http://www.philosophy-religion.org/handouts/pdfs/ch7-ethics.pdf, 120.
61. Stewart Fisher and Perry Martini, *Inspiring Leadership: Character and Ethics Matter* (Pennsylvania: Academy Leadership, 2004), 5.
62. William Hitt, *Ethics and Leadership: Putting Theory into Practice* (Ohio: Battelle Memorial Institute, 1990), 7.
63. William Hitt, *Ethics and Leadership: Putting Theory into Practice* (Ohio: Battelle Memorial Institute, 1990), 108.
64. Tom Beauchamp and Norman Bowie, *Ethical Theory and Business* (New Jersey: Pearson Education, Inc., 2004), 7.
65. Ibid, 7.
66. Gael McDonald, "Ethical Relativism Vs Absolutism: Research Implications." *European Business Review* 22, no. 4 (2010), 455.

67. Ibid, 455.
68. William H. Bishop, "The Role of Ethics in 21st Century Organizations." *Journal of Business Ethics* 118, no. 3 (12, 2013), 636.
69. Ibid, 636.
70. Keith Richburg, "Spitzer Linked to Prostitution Ring by Wiretap," *The Washington Post*, March 11, 2008, http://www.washingtonpost.com/wp-dyn/content/article/2008/03/10/AR2008031001482.html.
71. Ken Silverstein, "Enron, Ethics, and Today's Corporate Values," Forbes, May 14, 2013, http://www.forbes.com/sites/kensilverstein/2013/05/14/enron-ethics-and-todays-corporate-values/.
72. Ibid.
73. Ibid.
74. Alison Mitchell, "Impeachment: The Overview–Clinton Impeached: He Faces a Senate Trial, 2D in History: Vows to do Job Till Term's Last Hour," The New York Times, December 20, 1998, http://www.nytimes.com/1998/12/20/us/impeachment-overview-clinton-impeached-he-faces-senate-trial-2d-history-vows-job.html.
75. Julio Viskovich, "Unethical Behavior and Failure of Aig," *World Issues*, April 12, 2009, http://www.worldissues360.com/index.php/unethical-behavior-and-failure-of-aig-20316/.

76. David De Cremer, Ann E. Tenbrunsel, and Marius van Dijke, "Regulating Ethical Failures: Insights from Psychology." *Journal of Business Ethics* 95, (09, 2010), 1.
77. Jennell Evans, "Core Values: Wall Posters or Culture Builders?" *Psychology Today* (August 17, 2010) http://www.psychologytoday.com/blog/smartwork/201008/core-values-wall-posters-or-culture-builders
78. Camille Johnson, "It's All Relative," *Psychology Today* (June 29, 2012), http://www.psychologytoday.com/blog/its-all-relative/201206/unethical-behavior-can-become-contagious.
79. Marko Pitesa and Stefan Thau, "Compliant Sinners, Obstinate Saints: How Power and Self-focus Determine the Effectiveness of Social Influences in Ethical Decision Making." *Academy of Management Journal* 56, no. 3 (06, 2013), 635.
80. William H. Bishop, "The Role of Ethics in 21st Century Organizations." *Journal of Business Ethics* 118, no. 3 (12, 2013), 637.
81. Bruce Warren, Susan D. Sampson, and Erin McFee, "Business Schools: Ethics, Assurance of Learning, and the Future." *Organization Management Journal* 8, no. 1 (Spring, 2011), 41.
82. Shawn O'Connor, "The Responsibility of Business Schools in Training Ethical Leaders," *Forbes*

(May 15, 2013), http://www.forbes.com/sites/shawnoconnor/2013/05/15/the-responsibility-of-business-schools-in-training-ethical-leaders-2/.
83. Marko Pitesa and Stefan Thau, "Compliant Sinners, Obstinate Saints: How Power and Self-focus Determine the Effectiveness of Social Influences in Ethical Decision Making." *Academy of Management Journal* 56, no. 3 (06, 2013), 636.
84. Marko Pitesa and Stefan Thau, "Compliant Sinners, Obstinate Saints: How Power and Self-focus Determine the Effectiveness of Social Influences in Ethical Decision Making." *Academy of Management Journal* 56, no. 3 (06, 2013), 637.
85. Ibid, 637.
86. Thomas G. Ryan and Jeremy Bisson, "Can Ethics be Taught?" *International Journal of Business and Social Science* 2, no. 12 (07, 2011), 45.
87. "Rigell, Cicilline Introduce Bipartisan Bill to Establish Mandatory Ethics Training for Members of Congress," *The Rigell Report* http://rigell.house.gov/news/email/show.aspx?ID=YO74GLEARAZWTTMPZMG66WU4RM.,
88. LMU/LA, "Resolving an Ethical Dilemma," http://www.lmu.edu/Page27945.aspx.
89. Oxford English Dictionary online. http://www.oxforddictionaries.com/us/definition/american_english/utilitarianism.

90. Bernward Gesang, "Utilitarianism with a Human Face." *Journal of Value Inquiry* 39, no. 2 (2005), 169.
91. Paul Cleveland, "The Failure of Utilitarian Ethics in Political Economy," *The Independent Institute*, (September 1, 2002) http://www.independent.org/publications/article.asp?id=1602.
92. Julia Driver, "The History of Utilitarianism," *Stanford Encyclopedia of Philosophy* (March 27, 2009) http://plato.stanford.edu/entries/utilitarianism-history/.
93. Sophie Rietti, "Utilitarianism and Psychological Realism." *Utilitas* 21, no. 3 (09, 2009), 361.

Chapter 3

94. "Ethics and Morality," *Chapter 7*, http://www.philosophy-religion.org/handouts/pdfs/ch7-ethics.pdf, 120.
95. James Boice, *Genesis: An Expositional Commentary Volume 1* (Michigan: Zondervan, 1982), 203.
96. Edward Wilson, "The Biological Basis of Morality," *The Atlantic Online*, April 1998, https://www.theatlantic.com/past/docs/issues/98apr/biomoral.htm.
97. "Ethics and Morality," *Chapter 7*, http://www.philosophy-religion.org/handouts/pdfs/ch7-ethics.pdf, 118.

98. Frank Navran, "Defining Values, Morals, and Ethics," *Navran Associates,* www.navran.com/article-values-morals-ethics.html.
99. Frank Navran, "Defining Values, Morals, and Ethics," *Navran Associates,* www.navran.com/article-values-morals-ethics.html.
100. Christopher Kolenda, *Leadership: The Warrior's Art* (Pennsylvania: Army War College Foundation, 2001), 11.
101. Ibid, 12.
102. Steven Pinker, "The Moral Instinct," *The New York Times* (January 18, 2008) http://www.nytimes.com/2008/01/13/magazine/13Psychology-t.html?pagewanted=all&_r=0.
103. Jeffrey Kluger, "What Makes Us Moral," *Time,* November 21, 2007, http://content.time.com/time/specials/2007/article/0,28804,1685055_1685076_1686619-2,00.html.
104. Christopher Kolenda, *Leadership: The Warrior's Art* (Pennsylvania: Army War College Foundation, 2001), 12.
105. Eric Kail, "Leadership Character: The Role of Integrity," *The Washington Post* (July 8, 2011) http://www.washingtonpost.com/blogs/guest-insights/post/leadership-character-the-role-of-integrity/2011/04/04/gIQArZL03H_blog.html.

106. Blaine Fowers, "Defining Virtue," *Virtue and Psychology: Pursuing Excellence in Ordinary Practices* Washington, D.C.: American Psychology Association, 2005), 29.
107. Christopher Kolenda, *Leadership: The Warrior's Art* (Pennsylvania: Army War College Foundation, 2001), 12.
108. Ibid, 77.
109. Sankar, Y. "Character Not Charisma is the Critical Measures of Leadership Excellence." *Journal of Leadership & Organizational Studies* 9, no. 4 (Spring, 2003), 45.
110. Y. Sankar, "Character Not Charisma is the Critical Measures of Leadership Excellence." *Journal of Leadership & Organizational Studies* 9, no. 4 (Spring, 2003), 48.
111. Meghan Biro, "Are You a Character-Based Leader?" *Forbes* (September 30, 2012) http://www.forbes.com/sites/meghanbiro/2012/09/30/are-you-a-character-based-leader/.
112. Mary Crossan, Jeffrey Gandz, and Gerard Seijts, "Developing Leadership Character," *Ivey Business Journal* (January/February 2012) http://iveybusinessjournal.com/topics/leadership/developing-leadership-character#.U9O0E_2BBhN.
113. Mary Crossan, Jeffrey Gandz, and Gerard Seijts, "Developing Leadership Character," *Ivey Business*

Journal (January/February 2012) http://iveybusinessjournal.com/topics/leadership/developing-leadership-character#.U9O0E_2BBhN.

114. Abbas J. Ali, Manton Gibbs, and Robert C. Camp, "Human Resource Strategy: The Ten Commandments Perspective." *The International Journal of Sociology and Social Policy* 20, no. 5 (2000), 116.

115. Abbas J. Ali, Robert C. Camp, and Manton Gibbs, "The Ten Commandments Perspective on Power and Authority in Organizations." *Journal of Business Ethics* 26, no. 4 (08, 2000), 351.

116. "Ten Commandments," ACLJ, accessed July 13, 2014, http://aclj.org/church-state/ten-commandments.

117. Kenworthey Bilz and Janice Nadler, "Law, Psychology, and Morality," *Psychology of Learning and Motivation, Volume 50,* http://www.law.northwestern.edu/faculty/fulltime/nadler/Bilz_Nadler_Law.pdf, 102.

118. Kenworthey Bilz and Janice Nadler, "Law, Psychology, and Morality," *Psychology of Learning and Motivation, Volume 50,* http://www.law.northwestern.edu/faculty/fulltime/nadler/Bilz_Nadler_Law.pdf, 102.

119. Kenworthey Bilz and Janice Nadler, "Law, Psychology, and Morality," *Psychology of Learning and Motivation, Volume 50,* http://www.law.north-

western.edu/faculty/fulltime/nadler/Bilz_Nadler_Law.pdf, 103.
120. James Boice, "Is God's Word Sufficient for This Age?" *Alliance of Confessing Evangelicals* (1991).
121. Kenworthey Bilz and Janice Nadler, "Law, Psychology, and Morality," *Psychology of Learning and Motivation, Volume 50,* http://www.law.northwestern.edu/faculty/fulltime/nadler/Bilz_Nadler_Law.pdf, 108.
122. Kenworthey Bilz and Janice Nadler, "Law, Psychology, and Morality," *Psychology of Learning and Motivation, Volume 50,* http://www.law.northwestern.edu/faculty/fulltime/nadler/Bilz_Nadler_Law.pdf, 124.
123. "The Polis and Natural Law: The Moral Authority of the Urban Transect." http://www.frontporchrepublic.com/wp-content/uploads/2009/08/thepolisandnaturallaw.pdf, 6 &7.
124. "The Polis and Natural Law: The Moral Authority of the Urban Transect." http://www.frontporchrepublic.com/wp-content/uploads/2009/08/thepolisandnaturallaw.pdf, 6.
125. Nico P. Swartz and Obonye Jonas, "The Superiority or Integrity of Natural Law for our Time." *International Law Research* 1, no. 1 (2012), 120.
126. David van Drunen, "Natural Law and Christians in the Public Square," *Modern Reformation* (n.d.)

http://www.modernreformation.org/default.php?page=articledisplay&var2=93.

127. James Boice, *Romans: An Expositional Commentary, Volume I* (Michigan, Baker Books, 1991), 138.

128. Kathryn Lindskoog and G. Ellwood, "C.S. Lewis: Natural Law, the Law in Our Hearts," *Religion Online* (November 12, 1984) http://www.religion-online.org/showarticle.asp?title=1433.

129. Michael Stolleis and Lorraine Daston, 2008. *Natural Law and Laws of Nature in Early Modern Europe: Jurisprudence, Theology, Moral and Natural Philosophy.* Farnham, England: Ashgate Pub. Company, 2008. *eBook Collection (EBSCOhost)*, EBSCO*host* (accessed August 2, 2014), 75 & 76.

130. John Kleinsman, "Christian Moral Argument and Natural Law 'Faith and Reason' or 'Faith vs. Reason,'" *The Nathaniel Centre: New Zealand Catholic Bioethics Centre* (Issue 16, August 2005) http://www.nathaniel.org.nz/component/content/article/13-bioethical-issues/what-is-bioethics/128-christian-moral-argument-and-natural-law-qfaith-and-reasonq-or-qfaith-vs-reasonq.

131. Hasani Gittens, "High Times: The Next Five States to Tackle Pot Laws," *NBC News* (June 2, 2014) http://www.nbcnews.com/storyline/legal-

pot/high-times-next-five-states-tackle-pot-laws-n112321.
132. Anugrah Kumar, "Marriage is Not Priority for Millennials, Study Says," *Christian Post* (July 21, 2014) http://www.christianpost.com/news/marriage-is-not-priority-for-millennials-study-says-123586/.
133. Dan Johnson, "A Shift in Moral Authority." *The Futurist* 35, no. 6 (Nov, 2001), 18.
134. "Traditional Values Defined," *Traditional Value Coalition*, *http://www.traditionalvalues.org/content/defined*.
135. "How is Modern Day Christianity Morality Reconciled with the Morality of the Bible," *Christianity Stack Exchange, http://christianity.stackexchange.com/questions/8321/how-is-modern-day-christian-morality-reconciled-with-the-morality-of-the-bible*.
136. Dan Johnson, "A Shift in Moral Authority." *The Futurist* 35, no. 6 (Nov, 2001), 19.

Chapter 4

137. Authentic Leadership Development, http://www.hbs.edu/coursecatalog/2090.html.
138. Authentic Leadership Development, http://www.hbs.edu/coursecatalog/2090.html.
139. Peter Northouse, *Leadership: Theory and Practice* (California, Sage Publications, 2013), 258.

140. Lillian Cunningham, "Kentucky State President to Share His Salary with School's Lowest-Paid Workers," *The Washington Post* (August 5, 2014) http://www.washingtonpost.com/blogs/on-leadership/wp/2014/08/05/kentucky-state-president-to-share-his-salary-with-schools-lowest-paid-workers/.

141. Y. Sankar, "Character Not Charisma is the Critical Measures of Leadership Excellence." *Journal of Leadership & Organizational Studies* 9, no. 4 (Spring, 2003), 48.

142. Eric Kail, "Leadership Character: The Role of Integrity," *The Washington Post* (July 8, 2011) http://www.washingtonpost.com/blogs/guest-insights/post/leadership-character-the-role-of-integrity/2011/04/04/gIQArZL03H_blog.html.

143. Robert Moorman and Steven Grove, "Why Does Leader Integrity Matter to Followers? An Uncertainty Management-Based Explanation," *International Journal of Leadership Studies* (Vol. 5, Issue 2, 2009) http://www.regent.edu/acad/global/publications/ijls/new/vol5iss2/IJLS_vol5_iss2_moorman_grover_leader_integrity.pdf.

144. Robert Moorman and Steven Grove, "Why Does Leader Integrity Matter to Followers? An Uncertainty Management-Based Explanation," *International Journal of Leadership Studies* (Vol. 5, Issue 2,

2009) http://www.regent.edu/acad/global/publications/ijls/new/vol5iss2/IJLS_vol5_iss2_moorman_grover_leader_integrity.pdf, 107.

145. Robert Moorman and Steven Grove, "Why Does Leader Integrity Matter to Followers? An Uncertainty Management-Based Explanation," *International Journal of Leadership Studies* (Vol. 5, Issue 2, 2009) http://www.regent.edu/acad/global/publications/ijls/new/vol5iss2/IJLS_vol5_iss2_moorman_grover_leader_integrity.pdf, 109.

146. Bill George, "Wharton Interview: Authentic Leadership and Letting Your Strengths Bloom, *BillGeorge.org* (July 25, 2014) http://www.billgeorge.org/blog/.

147. William Bishop, "Defining the Authenticity in Authentic Leadership," *Journal of Values Based Leadership* (Winter/Spring 2013, Vol. 6, Issue 1), 2.

148. Corne Bekker (professor) in discussion with the author, May 2014.

149. Ronald Riggio, "What is Authentic Leadership? Do You Have It?" *Psychology Today* (January 22, 2014) http://www.psychologytoday.com/blog/cutting-edge-leadership/201401/what-is-authentic-leadership-do-you-have-it.

150. Bill George, Peter Sims, Andres McLean, and Diana Mayer, "Discovering Your Authentic Lead-

ership," *Harvard Business Review* (February 2007) http://www.aawccnatl.org/assets/authentic%20leadership.pdf, 4

151. William Bishop, "Defining the Authenticity in Authentic Leadership," *Journal of Values Based Leadership* (Winter/Spring 2013, Vol. 6, Issue 1), 4 & 5.
152. Susan Heitler, "Are You a Narcissist? 6 Sure Signs of Narcissism," *Psychology Today* (October 25, 2012) http://www.psychologytoday.com/blog/resolution-not-conflict/201210/are-you-narcissist-6-sure-signs-narcissism.
153. John Grohol, "Is Narcissism an Essential Leadership Trait?" *Psych Central.com* (January 16, 2014) http://psychcentral.com/news/2014/01/16/is-narcissism-an-essential-leadership-trait/64585.html.
154. Chelsey Coombs, "Narcissism – to a Point – Can Make a More Effective Leader, Researchers Find," *New Bureau Illinois* (Januar 15, 2014) http://news.illinois.edu/news/14/0115narcissism_EmilyGrijalva.html.
155. Michael Maccoby, "Narcissistic Leaders: The Incredible Pros, the Inevitable Cons," *Harvard Business Review* (January 2004) http://hbr.org/2004/01/narcissistic-leaders-the-incredible-pros-the-inevitable-cons/ar/1.

156. Jena McGregor, "Just the Right Level of Narcissism to be Successful," *The Washington Post* (January 22, 2014) http://www.washingtonpost.com/blogs/on-leadership/wp/2014/01/22/just-the-right-level-of-narcissism-to-be-successful/.
157. Michael Maccoby, "Narcissistic Leaders: The Incredible Pros, the Inevitable Cons." *Harvard Business Review* 82, no. 1 (January 2004): 92–101. *Business Source Complete*, EBSCO*host* (accessed August 24, 2014), 94.
158. Ibid.
159. Marjorie J. Cooper and Chris Pullig, "I'm Number One! Does Narcissism Impair Ethical Judgment Even for the Highly Religious?" *Journal of Business Ethics* 112, no. 1 (01, 2013), 167.
160. Kendra Cherry, "What is Groupthink?" *About.com Psychology* http://psychology.about.com/od/gindex/g/groupthink.htm.
161. Paul Hart, "Irving L. Janis' Victims of Groupthink," *Political Psychology*, Vol 12, No. 2, (1991) http://www.ftms.edu.my/pdf/Download/UndergraduateStudent/MOD%20000925%20Effective%20Team%20and%20Performance%20Management/Seminar%209-Janis%20-%20group%20think.pdf.

162. Ronald R. Sims, "Linking Groupthink to Unethical Behavior in Organizations." *Journal Of Business Ethics* 11, no. 9 (September 1992), 653.
163. Ronald R. Sims, "Linking Groupthink to Unethical Behavior in Organizations." *Journal Of Business Ethics* 11, no. 9 (September 1992), 660.

Chapter Five

164. John Maxwell, *The 21 Irrefutable Laws of Leadership* (Tennessee: Thomas Nelson, 2007), 13.
165. Bruce Winston and Kathleen Patterson, "An Integrative Definition of Leadership," *International Journal of Leadership Studies* Vol. 1 Issue 2, 2006, 7.
166. Peter Northouse, *Leadership: Theory and Practice* (California: Sage Publications, 2007), 3.
167. Kenneth Boulding, *Three Faces of Power* (California: Sage Publication, 1990), 65.
168. Peter Northouse, *Leadership: Theory and Practice* (California: Sage Publications, 2007), 7.
169. Kenneth Boulding, *Three Faces of Power* (California: Sage Publication, 1990), 25.
170. Kenneth Boulding, *Three Faces of Power* (California: Sage Publication, 1990), 25.
171. Kenneth Boulding, *Three Faces of Power* (California: Sage Publication, 1990), 27.
172. William Bishop, *Going Home: A Networking Survival Guide* (USA: Xulon Press, 2013) xvi.

173. Kenneth Boulding, *Three Faces of Power* (California: Sage Publication, 1990), 29.
174. S. K. Chakraborty and Pradip Bhattacharya, *Leadership and Power: Ethical Explorations* (New York: Oxford University Press, 2001), 20.
175. Venkat R. Krishnan, 2003. "Power and Moral Leadership: Role of Self-Other Agreement." *Leadership & Organization Development Journal* 24 (5): 345.
176. Ibid.
177. Ibid.
178. Ibid.
179. Ibid.
180. Paula Braynion, 2004. "Power and Leadership." *Journal of Health Organization and Management* 18 (6), 449–450.
181. Robert Wilson, "Leadership vs. Power," *Psychology Today* (December 31, 2009) http://www.psychologytoday.com/blog/the-main-ingredient/200912/leadership-vs-power.
182. Jun Liu, Xiaoyu Liu, and Xianju Zeng. "Does Transactional Leadership Count for Team Innovativeness?" *Journal of Organizational Change Management* 24, no. 3 (2011), 284.
183. A. G. Stone, Robert F. Russell, and Kathleen Patterson, "Transformational versus Servant Leadership: A

Difference in Leader Focus." *Leadership & Organization Development Journal* 25, no. 3 (2004), 350.
184. Ibid.
185. Mark A. Papworth, Derek Milne, and George Boak, "An Exploratory Content Analysis of Situational Leadership." *The Journal of Management Development* 28, no. 7 (2009), 594.
186. Peter Northouse, *Leadership: Theory and Practice* (California: Sage Publications, 2007), 152.
187. Ibid, 154.
188. Ibid.
189. Erich C. Fein, Aharon Tziner, Liat Lusky, and Ortal Palachy, "Relationships between Ethical Climate, Justice Perceptions, and LMX." *Leadership & Organization Development Journal* 34, no. 2 (2013), 157.
190. Kevin S. Groves and Michael A. Larocca, "An Empirical Study of Leader Ethical Values, Transformational and Transactional Leadership, and Follower Attitudes Toward Corporate Social Responsibility." *Journal of Business Ethics* 103, no. 4 (11, 2011), 513.
191. Kevin S. Groves and Michael A. Larocca, "An Empirical Study of Leader Ethical Values, Transformational and Transactional Leadership, and Follower Attitudes Toward Corporate Social

Responsibility." *Journal of Business Ethics* 103, no. 4 (11, 2011), 512.
192. Marty McMahone, "Servant Leadership as a Teachable Ethical Concept." *American Journal of Business Education (Online)* 5, no. 3 (2012), 341.
193. Lora L. Reed, Deborah Vidaver-Cohen, and Scott R. Colwell, "A New Scale to Measure Executive Servant Leadership: Development, Analysis, and Implications for Research." *Journal of Business Ethics* 101, no. 3 (07, 2011), 416.
194. Marty McMahone, "Servant Leadership as a Teachable Ethical Concept." *American Journal of Business Education (Online)* 5, no. 3 (2012), 340.
195. Ibid, 343.
196. Uma D. Jogulu and Glenice J. Wood, "The Role of Leadership Theory in Raising the Profile of Women in Management." *Equal Opportunities International* 25, no. 4 (2006), 245.
197. Ibid.
198. Joanne Lubline and Kelly Eggers, "More Women Are Primed to Land CEO Roles," *Wall Street Journal* (April 30, 2012) http://online.wsj.com/news/articles/SB10001424052702303990604577368344256435440.
199. James Ike Schaap, "Who Wants Power More: Men or Women?" *Advances in Management and Applied Economics* 4, no. 1 (2014), 160.

200. Sebastian C. Schuh, Alina Hernandez Barks, Niels Van Quaquebeke, Rüdiger Hossiep, Philip Frieg, and Rolf Van Dick, "Gender Differences in Leadership Role Occupancy: The Mediating Role of Power Motivation." *Journal of Business Ethics* 120, no. 3 (03, 2014), 364.
201. Margaret M. Hopkins, Deborah A. O'Neil, and Diana Bilimoria, "Effective Leadership and Successful Career Advancement: Perspectives from Women in Health Care." *Equal Opportunities International* 25, no. 4 (2006), 253.
202. Adler, Nancy J. Adler, "Global Leadership: Women Leaders." *Management International Review* 37, no. 1 (1997), 187–188.
203. Glenn Llopis, "The Most Undervalued Leadership Traits of Women," *Forbes* (February 2, 2014) http://www.forbes.com/sites/glennllopis/2014/02/03/the-most-undervalued-leadership-traits-of-women/.

Epilogue

204. Kim Cameron and Robert Quinn, *Diagnosing and Changing Organizational Culture Based on the Competing Values Framework.* (California: Jossey-Bass, 2011), 44.
205. Kim Cameron and Robert Quinn, *Diagnosing and Changing Organizational Culture Based on the*

Competing Values Framework. (California: Jossey-Bass, 2011), 46, 48.
206. Kim Cameron and Robert Quinn, *Diagnosing and Changing Organizational Culture Based on the Competing Values Framework.* (California: Jossey-Bass, 2011), 45.

ABOUT THE AUTHOR

William Bishop is the chief executive officer and founder of the Bishop Advisory Group, a consulting company that harnesses the power of critical thinking to provide practical solutions to global challenges. He is a veteran of the United States Navy, where he ascended to the rank of chief petty officer in seven years. While a doctoral student at Regent University, Dr. Bishop pioneered and promulgated the concept of servant networking. Bill is a prolific author, whose works have been featured in Talent Management, the Journal of Strategic Leadership, Proceedings, the Journal of Values Based Leadership, and Leadership Advance Online. He holds degrees from Excelsior College (BS), Regent University (MBA, DSL), and is a graduate of Harvard Business School's Executive Education Program (Authentic Leadership Development). www.bishopadvisorygroup.com